Voices in Flight:
The Dambuster
Squadron

Voices in Flight: The Dambuster Squadron

Colin Higgs and Bruce Vigar

Pen & Sword
AVIATION

First published in Great Britain in 2013 by
PEN & SWORD AVIATION
an imprint of
Pen & Sword Books Ltd
47 Church Street
Barnsley
South Yorkshire
S70 2AS

ISBN 978-1-78159-371-4

A CIP catalogue record for this book is available from the British Library.

Printed ar   , Victoria Square,
kshire.

Pen & Swor   & Sword Aviation,
Pen & Swor   ı & Sword Military,
Pen & Swor   rncliffe True Crime,
Wharncliff   d Military Classics,
Leo Cooper, The Praetorian Press, Remember When, Seaforth Publishing and Frontline Publishing.

For a complete list of Pen & Sword titles please contact
PEN & SWORD BOOKS LIMITED
47 Church Street, Barnsley, South Yorkshire, S70 2AS, England
E-mail: enquiries@pen-and-sword.co.uk
Website: www.pen-and-sword.co.uk

Contents

List of Plates

The famous photograph of Guy Gibson and his crew before setting off on the Dams raid on the evening of 16 May 1943.

ED825, AJ-T. George Johnson attacked the Sorpe Dam in this aircraft flown by Joe McCarthy.

An Upkeep 'bouncing bomb' attached to Guy Gibson's aircraft, AJ-G, before the Dams raid.

King George VI inspecting photographs taken after the Dams raid with Guy Gibson and Air Commodore Whitworth.

Guy Gibson with a large aerial photograph of the Möhne Dam taken after the Dams raid.

Grant McDonald with other Canadian and American aircrew who survived the Dams raid.

Survivors of the Dams raid photographed at a celebration dinner given by A.V. Roe at the Hungaria Restaurant in Regent Street, London, on 22 June 1943, the same day they had been to the Palace for the investiture.

617 Squadron photograph taken on 9 July 1943, a few days before Wing Commander Guy Gibson left the squadron.

Leonard Cheshire, Officer Commanding 617 Squadron from September 1943 to July 1944.

Famous trio of photographs of target indicators dropped by Leonard Cheshire at very low level over the Gnome-Rhône aero-engine factory at Limoges on 8 February 1944.

Crater created by a 12,000lb Tallboy which destroyed the V-2 rocket site at Wizernes in France on 17 July 1944.

Wing Commander James Tait DSO*** DFC* who commanded 617 Squadron from July to December 1944 and led the attack that sank the *Tirpitz*.

John Bell.
Tom Bennett.
Frank Tilley.
Benny Goodman.
Murray Valentine.
Murray Valentine, Benny Goodman, and John Langston.

Acknowledgements

When we set out to conduct our first ever filmed interview many years ago little did we realise that by 2013 we would have spent so many wonderful days recording the stories of veterans from all over the world. Initially the interviews were arranged for inclusion in specific documentaries destined either for TV or home video release. After a while, we realised that these interviews were so enlightening, so valuable and so full of humour, anecdote and memory that we really had to get as many as possible 'in the can'.

So our first thanks go to the many veterans who have allowed us into their homes to 'grill' them on their wartime experiences. For this book in particular we would like to thank the men of 617 Squadron, and their families, for such insight into their lives at that time.

As the interviews were originally planned for inclusion in programmes we would like to thank Charles Hewitt of Pen & Sword for publishing a book that allows us to use almost all of each interview rather than just the short clips that would have been used for TV. Also thanks go to Paula Hurst, Laura Hirst and Richard Doherty for guiding us through the minefield of writing our first book.

There are many other people who deserve our thanks for their assistance in getting this book from an idea to reality: Gary Rushbrooke for his enthusiasm and support throughout the project; Tim Prince, and previously David Higham, from RIAT and the Royal Air Force Charitable Trust Enterprises, who helped us to contact many of the veterans; Colin Hudson and Caroline Fowler from Aces High Gallery in Wendover who have persuaded veterans that we are 'good guys' and can be allowed into their homes; Mike Jowett for allowing us to use his photographs also courtesy of Aces High; Jo Ware for her expert indexing; and Beverley Higgs for accurately transcribing hours of recorded interview and providing excellent critical analysis.

Authors' Preface

Voices In Flight: The Dambuster Squadron is based on interviews with those who served on 617 Squadron, Royal Air Force, from its inception in March 1943 to the end of the Second World War. The accounts cover the big missions: the Dams raid, *Tirpitz*, Bielefeld Viaduct and others but they also paint a vivid picture of life in a front-line bomber squadron during the Second World War. Because these are personal accounts rather than cold histories, what and why certain events and details are recalled more vividly than others is down to how the individuals regarded them. The accounts are about what mattered to them.

All the accounts have been taken from recorded interviews. These interviews have then been transcribed and edited. Wherever possible, the historical accuracy of the accounts has been checked. But it may be that the passage of time means that some names, places or times are inaccurate. Apart from occasional interlinking sentences, the accounts are in their own words.

The rank given at the start of each chapter and on the contents page is the highest attained by the interviewee whilst on the squadron.

Each account is a chapter. Where possible, they have been arranged chronologically but there are inevitable overlaps.

In its seventieth anniversary year 617 Squadron is possibly the most famous squadron in the Royal Air Force because of the men and their comrades featured in this book. As their numbers dwindle to a handful of survivors these accounts reveal something of how that reputation was forged.

Colin Higgs
Bruce Vigar
2013

Foreword

In March 1943 I was a bomb-aimer on Flight Lieutenant Joe McCarthy's crew in 97 Squadron. We were just completing our first tour of operations and were about to go on leave. Later that month Joe called us together and said that he had been asked by Wing Commander Guy Gibson to join a 'special squadron' he was forming for just one trip. We readily agreed to join him and on 27 March we transferred from Woodhall to Scampton to join Squadron X – later to be renamed 617 Squadron.

A series of surprises presented themselves on arrival. A number of highly experienced crews were assembling. Clearly this was no ordinary gathering. All training was to be done at low level – 100 feet was the prescribed level but it was seldom adhered to and 60 feet was a lot more interesting. We were not told what the target would be and there was the strictest security about everything we were doing. There were many guesses about the target but it was still not until the final briefing that we understood what the specific training had been for. One could not help but be impressed by the determination of all the crews and the ready acceptance of onerous security and rigorous training. All bomber crews were, and are, dependent upon strong relationships between the crew members. A belief that everyone would do their job. A reliance on each other to act with skill and discipline. Much is written about the importance of leadership and in this context I would like to endorse that view. I had supreme confidence in my pilot, Big Joe. It stayed with me throughout my time on his crew and blossomed into post-war friendship. Later I would serve under Wing Commander Cheshire and he was the finest commander I experienced in my operational career.

One of my abiding memories of the Dams raid was on our return from our target. We passed over what was left of the Möhne Dam. The sight of that inland sea, with water still pouring out of the Dam, gave us tremendous satisfaction as to what had been achieved. The personal disappointment was that only one other aircraft had got through to the Sorpe Dam and it had not been breached. There was also the sad fact that the raid cost the lives of so many of our colleagues, a fact which caused Sir Barnes Wallis great distress.

Writing this Foreword nearly seventy years after the event I am aware that a high level of interest in the raid remains. Much has been written, filmed and televised about the attack. I am equally aware that the reputation of the original squadron has been maintained by those who have followed in our footsteps. They too have made their mark in the best traditions of the Royal Air Force in many areas of conflict around the world and in some cases some have also made the supreme sacrifice.

I take much pride in their achievements. Seventy years on 617 remains a 'special squadron'.

George 'Johnny' Johnson
February 2013

Chapter 1

Squadron Leader Les Munro

John Leslie 'Les' Munro CNZM DSO QSO DFC JP was born in Gisborne, New Zealand, on 5 April 1919. The son of a farmer, Les Munro enlisted in the Royal New Zealand Air Force in 1941. Originally he had been turned down as not being sufficiently qualified but, with the determination that later came to define his career, he completed his studies by correspondence and was finally accepted.

I have a rather conservative nature as I was brought up in the country and with a rather staid father. We never indulged in social activities in my youth. In fact I was brought up in the slump and we couldn't afford to go to parties or go out to drink and that sort of thing. I worked on a farm for the eighteen months before I volunteered so I was a probably a bit different to the ordinary. Oh, I occasionally would go out but we used to indulge in ordinary games in the mess afterwards but I didn't hit it up much.

I went through quite an intensive and extensive period of training which took place almost eighteen months before I actually was posted to 97 Squadron.

Despite the urgent need for aircrew in one of the most active and dangerous phases of the air war, the need for thorough training wasn't compromised and, as Les explains, could take a considerable time.

I've often asked myself why it took so long because losses were pretty heavy in 1941, and even the beginning of '42, and I find it rather surprising that it took me eighteen months to reach operations. I joined the air force on 7 July 1941 and trained on Tiger Moths in New Zealand off New Plymouth. I went to Canada and trained on Cessna planes at Saskatoon in the province of Saskatchewan. It was the middle of winter and the whole country-side was covered in snow and the only evidence of buildings you could see was the plumes of smoke coming from the housing. Subsequently, I came to England and after a period in a holding paddock at Bournemouth I was posted to Shawbury for a short period. I did a refresher course on Airspeed Oxfords where I did an extensive number of hours on link trainers and simulated night-flying conditions and instrument flying. From there I went to 29 OTU [Operational Training Unit] at North Luffenham where I flew Wellingtons. I took part in the first one of the early [Thousand] bomber raids where aircraft from operational training units cooperated to make up numbers. From there I went to 1654 Heavy Conversion Unit and flew Manchesters for a few flights and then onto the Lancaster before being posted to 97 Squadron on 12 December 1942.

At operational training in North Luffenham I got my navigator, bomb-aimer, and wireless operator and rear gunner. When I went to the heavy conversion unit I got the flight engineer and mid upper gunner.

The first bomb-aimer I had suffered from altitude sickness or oxygen sickness – unfortunately he passed out on the bombing run. So, that really created real complications and after two incidents I said that he was to be taken off operations. While I stayed on 97 Squadron I think I had six or eight different bomb aimers. On 617 of course I was given another bomb-aimer and he stayed with me right very nearly to the end of my operations.

I think it's important that a crew operates as a unit; they fly as a unit and they trust each other and develop a spirit of camaraderie. It was important to me as a Captain and also for completing successful operations.

I felt that as I progressed from Cessna planes in Canada to Airspeed Oxfords in Shawbury, to Wellingtons at North Luffenham, you sort of crept up the ladder a little bit. From a point of view of size and power of the various aircraft and the transition from twin engine Wellingtons through the Manchester, that period actually prepared me, because a Manchester was the same, more or less, as the Lancaster but with two [fewer] engines. So, it was a natural progression from twin engine, a large twin engine plane to a four-engine plane. I had no difficulty at all in transferring or carrying on from one plane to another.

Like so many other Bomber Command crewmen Les Munro has a special affection for the Avro Lancaster.

I've always felt a great deal of pride in the fact that I flew Lancasters during the war. I have a great deal of admiration for it; it was a wonderful plane to fly. I think it was an attacking weapon; it was probably one of the best as far as the bombers were concerned. It could carry a terrific bomb load. Maybe it could not withstand as much damage as the geodetic construction of the Wellington but it could sustain quite a bit of damage from light flak providing it was not too close. We had numerous occasions where we were peppered with fragments of light flak without causing any serious damage. But as a fighting weapon I think, yes, it was probably the best the Allies had.

I had occasion to look up my log book recently and I think the highest I've bombed from was 24,500 feet. And the Lancaster could achieve those heights – 20,000 or 22,000 was commonplace for bombing when I was on 97 Squadron. Of course, we would try and gain height after having bombed, to climb as high as possible to get above the range of fighters and, from memory, 28,500 feet [was the highest]. Again, it demonstrates its ability as an all-round aircraft. It never had any problem taking off with a heavy bomb load. The power of the four Merlins was quite significant and a major factor in the performance of the Lancaster during the war.

I think it took it [the variety of bomb loads carried during the war] in its stride. I think probably if you compared it to later on with the 22,000-pounder, the 10-ton bomb, that would have had a major impact on its aerodynamics and that sort of thing, its ability to fly. But the transition from ordinary bombs to the Tallboy was achieved without any difficulty. I think if you had a short distance to the target and we had a heavy bomb load, there was probably a slight requirement for more power. But on the whole the Lancaster took that sort of thing in its stride.

Finally, in December 1942, Les Munro was posted to his first operational squadron, 97 Squadron, which had begun the war flying Handley Page Heyfords. The Heyford was an older, 1930s, design of heavy biplane bomber which only ever equipped twelve RAF squadrons during its operational life. Soon after the Heyford was retired from service 97 Squadron was disbanded in April 1940. Reformed in

February 1941 No. 97 Squadron was equipped with the new Avro Manchester twin-engine bomber.

Constant overheating and unreliability problems with the Rolls Royce Vulture engines meant that the Manchester's operational life came to a premature end and 97 Squadron became just the second RAF squadron to be equipped with the new four-engine Avro Lancaster bomber.

Now Les was to find out whether all the training and all the waiting had been worthwhile.

Whether you could say it prepared me for actual operations I'm not that sure about that. That actually comes with undertaking operations and to gain that feeling of danger and that sort of thing. But certainly from the point of view of my ability as a pilot I think it did prepare me.

Well, the first trip went particularly well, we had no problems. The second, two nights later, we took off and I had the misfortune to crash the aircraft just after take-off without any injury to any of the crew. That was the first evidence that lady luck was going to be on my shoulder for the rest of the war because we all escaped and the plane caught fire and all the 500-pounders we had blew up.

You always felt a sort of junior 'sprog'. I personally didn't feel any different after all the flying I had done in previous months in undertaking my first mission. The first mission was a mining operation. It was probably the only operation throughout the war that I felt fear, for some unknown reason. It was an innocuous sort of an operation, mining at the mouth of the Gironde river. We arrived down there and we were circling round prior to dropping the mines. The outline of the French coast looked dark and ominous and I'm not sure that we really were positive that we were in the right spot. For some reason I had a touch of fear and I've never been able to explain it, except that the French coast looked ominous in the darkness and that sort of thing. I never had occasion to feel that fear again right through the war. But a couple of nights later I did another mining trip without any problems. And then we progressed to ordinary bombing raids. I saw my place as a junior member of the squadron although my rank was Flight Lieutenant by the time I'd done a few trips and a lot of the junior officers were flying officers, pilot officers and that sort of thing. I don't remember feeling out of place, put it that way.

Out of those first three or four or five operations I think I did two on Berlin and two on Essen so I was thrown straight into the thick of it. On those particular raids, I'm not sure what the weather conditions were like but certainly as time went on in 97 we were operating in the middle of winter and operating in ten tenths cloud so you didn't have the visual effect of what was going on, on the ground underneath. You'd be flying across a city that's lit up by flares and searchlights and flak bursting in the sky and all that sort of thing. It was not dramatic to me; I think the crew took it in their stride. Except I must say on the second Berlin trip my wireless operator decided to come out and have a look at what was going on over the city. Berlin was in no cloud and we had this large concentration of fires, flak bursting everywhere and white searchlights waving and he came out and had a look and he said, 'Jesus Christ have we come through that?' and you know the old saying: what you don't see you don't worry about. Good illustration I think of that saying.

Of all the sorties regularly carried out by Bomber Command it was the targets in the industrial region of the Ruhr, or 'Happy Valley' as it became known, that were among the most feared. Much of Germany's industrial production was centred round the cities bordered by the rivers Ruhr, Rhine and Lippe, and hundreds of bombers were sent out night after night to attack Essen, Mulheim, Hamm, Dortmund, Duisburg and many more.

The Battle of the Ruhr was a five-month-long bombing campaign that began in March 1943. Les Munro was well into his first tour, and had already flown two trips to Essen and two to Cologne when the campaign started. So with more experience than most pilots Les was perhaps more qualified to cope with the challenges of operations to 'Happy Valley'.

The Ruhr was always recognised as being heavily defended and that was one of the concerns when we saw the targets for the Dams raid up on the map, that the routes led through the Ruhr and that was a recognised heavily defended area with large concentrations of flak. The Ruhr was not a happy hunting ground for bomber crews.

I think for those crews that had been operating for some time, they got to know the worst, the most heavily defended towns. They got to know the state of the defences. The first thing they'd do is look up on the briefing room, look at where the tapes led to. The crews would evaluate and make a quick decision as to how difficult it was going to be. How the overall operation was going to be: not too bad or pretty grim by the town or the city we were going to bomb.

The Ruhr provided many dangers for the bombers. It was still winter when the campaign began in March. The importance of the factories in the area meant that it was one of the most well-defended areas in Europe. And the industrial production meant that there was a continuous smog, or haze, hanging over the targets. Despite gaining more and more experience it was still difficult to complete an operation successfully.

I think the difference there would be in the ability of the bomb-aimer to pick up the target, the aiming points. And it would be largely dependent on his ability to be able to identify the target, the bombing point or the aiming point from the rest of the city. The introduction of flares and target markers was certainly a big help. But they weren't always a hundred per cent successful. Sometimes they were wide of the target area.

You started off as you approached the city. You were guided by the navigator to start with as to the exact route to take. Within near proximity of the city the bomb-aimer took over. The bomb-aimer directed the pilot. He identified the target through his bomb-sight and he guided the pilot left or right. Of course you should have been flying at your pre-determined height or whatever the course as assessed by navigator. But the bomb-aimer then had the control of the aircraft over the target area and he would be working through his bomb-sight, tracking towards the target. When he reached the aiming point on his bomb-sight then he said bombs gone and you were away. Close the bomb doors and take off again on a pre-determined course. Once you were clear of the city you were in the hands of the navigator.

One of the danger points of a bombing raid was while you were on that straight course over a target. Probably the most dangerous part of the operation was when you were doing your bombing run.

I was never attacked by a night-fighter. Only occasionally was I caught with searchlights. The problem with the searchlight was if one battery of searchlights caught a plane and illuminated it the German searchlight batteries tended to focus on that and you had a great deal of difficulty escaping that. If they flicked past you and if you took quick evasive action you wouldn't be caught again. But I don't think I was ever coned by a number of searchlights. It would have been very difficult in a Lancaster to escape a cone unless you lost height very, very quickly and you wouldn't do that with a bomb load of course.

It depended largely on what cloud cover there was of course. But if there was no cloud cover and you were flying at 20,000 feet you could see for a long distance ahead. It would be a glow in the sky at long distance and gradually increasing in size the nearer you got to the target.

Flying high level bombing operations in the winter could cause many physical challenges to the crew as well as problems for the aircraft.

I used Irvin trousers quite often. They kept you pretty warm and you wore silk gloves and outer gloves. I never ever found the cold in a Lancaster a major disadvantage. I always felt for the gunners a little bit in their turrets but again, they had electrical systems to plug into for their flying suits.

Occasionally if the conditions were right we did ice up. That caused problems with a lot of aircraft. I didn't have any occasions where icing affected the ability of the plane to carry on flying.

However, icing up did affect the release systems on the bombs and, on one occasion, I had a bomb hang up until we got back to the North Sea. And on one occasion we had a 500-pounder rolling around in the bomb bay. The bomb doors themselves would freeze up and it wasn't until we're down long enough at low level for the ice to melt for the bomb bays to be able to open and we would be able to drop or jettison whatever bombs had not been released over the target. On one occasion I got back to Woodhall, I was still on 97, and it was normal practice when you were taxiing round the perimeter track, to get back to your marshalling point to open the bomb bay. On this occasion, half a dozen incendiaries dropped out onto the perimeter track and caught fire. That was another indication of what might happen when you got iced up.

Barnes Wallis was an inventor and engineer who had been instrumental in airship design from before the First World War before being recruited to become a vital part of the Vickers Armstrong design team at Weybridge in Surrey. One of Wallis' ideas resulted in the Wellington bomber which became the mainstay of RAF Bomber Command in the early years of the war. But Wallis did not just concentrate on aircraft design. Like many great inventors before him Barnes Wallis combined imagination and inspiration with outstanding engineering knowledge. The diversity and scope of his ideas was so impressive but were sometimes best applied to specific practical problems that particular targets posed. Much of German industrial production was dispersed over wide areas making it virtually impossible to destroy more than a small percentage by conventional bombing methods but there were certain targets which couldn't move and be dispersed. And they included dams. Before the war the Air Ministry and Bomber Command had both considered that the destruction of major dams near the Ruhr could have a devastating effect. It was Barnes Wallis, however, who came up with the practical solution of how to do it.

Wallis came up with the idea of a bomb, or more accurately a mine, that could be dropped from low level, skip along the surface of the water, lodge against the wall of the dam and explode as it sank into the water.

Bomber Command fully supported Wallis' ideas and decided that a special squadron was needed. On 1 April 1943 No. 617 Squadron was officially formed. It had a single purpose, one operation - to destroy three of the dams of western Germany, flood the Ruhr valley and disrupt industrial production.

Les Munro and his crew were among the first accepted to join 617 Squadron.

It was voluntary, movement to 617. Gibson didn't select the pilots. He may have selected a few from his 106 Squadron. But all 5 Group bomber squadrons were circulated with a letter from headquarters calling for volunteers from crews nearing the end of their first tour of operations or thirty trips and from crews commencing their second. That time I'd done twenty-one operational trips and I discussed with my crew whether we should volunteer or not. They agreed that we should and so I was a volunteer. I don't believe I was in any way selected to go because of my past experience or anything like that. But having volunteered I was accepted as one of the new crews to form this new squadron.

Volunteers were called for to form a new squadron for a special operation, that's all we knew and all we were told. Even over nearly all of the training period we weren't actually told the target.

The opportunity to indulge in authorised low flying was a real boon. Most pilots enjoyed low flying – well not all I suppose, but most would enjoy low flying and of course it was taboo to low fly unless authorised. The opportunity to undertake low flying on a continual basis over the training period was accepted with a great deal of satisfaction from pilots.

I think there was a lot of guessing [about what the target would be] but it wasn't done very openly. I can't remember discussing at any particular time what the target might be. No doubt we did. But the opportunity to fly, I enjoyed it. I think most pilots did. The exhilaration of low flying [for] 220 miles is great, providing you can become competent at gauging how far ahead obstacles are and being able to pull up to clear them. That was a major factor in the pilot's competence and of course if you didn't pull up quick enough then you hit whatever. There were a number of occasions in those early stages that pilots would come back with twigs and leaves in their air intakes and that sort of thing. I've never known how many pilots actually were guilty of that but it certainly happened. And that was what the expertise of low flying came back to: that ability to assume or to judge how close you were and when you should clear that obstacle.'

One of the first jobs for the crew was to get to know their new Commanding Officer, Wing Commander Guy Gibson.

It's a question I don't really enjoy answering. I try and describe him as what I imagine a peacetime officer would have been, in the discipline of peacetime. He was an authoritarian and he didn't suffer fools gladly. If he gave an order he expected people to carry it out. He didn't brook arguments. But in the Mess, off duty, he liked to be one of the boys, very sociable. But on duty he was very strict. He was alright as a leader. I think as a leader, particularly on the operation itself, he did a great job.

We were warned right from the start that security was to be a major issue. Gibson made the point that any relaxation in security would be severely dealt with because of the importance of the target of which we were still unaware. I don't think I ever left the squadron, in training for 617 so it wasn't a factor as far as I was concerned. I can't remember whether any of my crew ever went off station during the training period. But it was a major issue as far as general standards of behaviour were concerned.

We gathered in the Mess after the first day with all the crews and to look around and see all these aircrew with campaign medals and DFCs and DSOs really indicated that here was a group of pilots and crews who were really experienced and obviously picked for what was to be a most difficult target.

Twelve aircraft took part in the trials of the bombs and it was over the eleventh, twelfth and thirteenth of May. Six of those were badly damaged through splash. I was one of the guilty ones but I can't remember whether I was too low or too high. My rear gunner was jammed in his turret and he wasn't able to get back until we landed back at base. But not quite as bad as perhaps Henry Maudsley's plane that was damaged and I don't think that one flew again – for the raid I mean.

It [the training] was intense, mainly because we were at it day after day after day. I think I was pretty good at low flying and I never had any problems with it. I was able to fly pretty low at less than 50 feet on most occasions, treetop height and even below treetop height was a common occurrence. I think that in that type of flying I was alright.

We undertook cross-country flights almost daily and about three or four air flights. Most of them incorporated flying over Derwent Water or the Uppingham Reservoir and one or two subsidiary dams that I don't really remember. I do remember quite clearly the times I flew over the Derwent water and then we'd go north and then come down the North Sea and home that way. We always incorporated some low level bombing training at Wainfleet. On those flights concentration was on all members of the crew being able to undertake visual navigation, being able to identify targets while approaching at low level at 220 or 230 miles per hour. And you can appreciate, flying at 10,000, 15,000 or 20,000 feet, visual navigation is quite simple because you can see so many miles ahead and you can explore the horizon and pick up landmarks relatively easily whereas at low level, flying 50 or 60 feet, they are there before you know you're on them. So, as the pilot was busy flying the plane, the bomb-aimer and the navigator and the gunners had to become experienced at identifying targets very quickly – made all the more difficult of course when we were doing it at night.

Finally the training was over and it was time for the crews to learn exactly what it had all been for.

The first I knew was when we walked into the briefing room, late afternoon on the day of the operation. I think the day before Gibson and the two flight commanders, the bombing leader and the navigation leader had been briefed. Whether the two flight commanders had been in the picture before that, the day before main briefing I don't know, I somehow doubt that on the grounds of security. So when we walked into the briefing room and saw the target I think the main concern was the fact that the routes led up over the Ruhr valley. Most of us were aware that was probably the most defended area in Germany. That was the concern rather than any concern that might have been raised by the fact that we were going to bomb dams and not buildings and infrastructure.

The aircraft were fitted with hydraulic arms that were attached to the side of the aircraft and swung outwards and they were clamped over each end of the Upkeep [Codename for Wallis' bouncing bomb].

With the Upkeep, as compared to the conventional bombs, there was a certain amount of extra drag because the Upkeep was situated across the aircraft. There was a wallowing effect on the aircraft while flying, trying to maintain height with the Upkeep spinning at 500 revs a minute.

Once you knew how it operated, the fact that it was spinning was a real departure from normal convention. I remember the first time on a test drop, we spun it at 500 revs a minute and that really had an effect. You could feel the effect of 9,250 pounds revolving.

It caused a juddering effect and it did affect lift to a certain extent. But on the whole the Lancaster coped with it pretty well.

The operation took place on the night of the 16/17 May 1943. There was very little other activity that night so the skies over Europe were quiet.

Les was in the second wave tasked with attacking the Sorpe Dam.

I was one of five aircraft that were flying due East from Lincolnshire to a spot above the island of Vlieland. The first nine aircraft led by Guy Gibson went further south. We turned right to go down south down across the Waddenzee and Zuiderzee and joined the same route down somewhere round about Hamm that Gibson's nine aircraft had taken. So I turned at our turning point and approached the island of Vlieland and I could see the breakers ahead as we approached the island's foreshore and the sand dunes above the level of the sea. I gained a certain amount of height just to clear them. I must have been flying pretty low, about 30 or 40 feet, something like that, and I had actually cleared the top of the dunes and was losing height on the other side when a line of tracer appeared on the port side and we were hit by one shell amidships. It cut all the communication and electrical systems and everything went dead. I asked the wireless operator if he would inspect the damage and see whether it could be repaired. In the meantime I was circling round in the Zuiderzee. When he came back and said 'no', and at that stage we were communicating by lifting the flaps of our flying helmets virtually yelling at each other's ears, and when he came back and said 'no' it couldn't be repaired I made the decision to return to base. The absolutely essential navigation would have been extremely difficult without being able to communicate with the navigator and with the crew being able to identify targets. And even if we'd got to the target, how would the bomb-aimer have been able to direct me as pilot on the run up to the dam? I believe I had no alternative and reluctantly it was my decision to go back and had the dubious distinction of being the first one to land with a live bomb.

No orders were ever given that we were not to bring it (the bomb) back. No orders given that we were to jettison in the sea. I am quite adamant in that. The question I would pose is if that was the case, if there was any danger, why would I as a captain of the crew put my own life and those of my crew in danger by bringing it back? Simple as that.

Les and his crew landed at thirty minutes past midnight, three hours after take-off.

Well, we would have reported of course after getting back to headquarters. We would have been debriefed on what happened and then I think we just went back to our respective messes and awaited the outcome of the operation. I was rather embarrassed because here were these blokes who'd got to the target and took part in the actual bombing and I didn't do that, I didn't achieve that and it was somewhat embarrassing for me to participate in the festivities that went on. Those festivities of course were tinged with sadness and regret by the fact that eight crews weren't coming back, that was a sad blow to the squadron as a whole.

When I volunteered for 617 Squadron I never dreamt that I would become part of history. After the Dams raid we just carried on training. Nobody seemed to know what they were going to do with the squadron that had been formed for a special purpose. We did those shuttle raids to Italy. They called them shuttle raids because we went on to land in North Africa and came back on another one. We bombed transformer stations on one raid, went on, and bombed Leghorn [Livorno] on the way back.

I think we were all frustrated the fact that we were doing nothing but training and not knowing what we were going to do next and this sort of thing. It was quite enjoyable to get back on actual operations and that was an experience in itself having to carry on and land and spend time in Blida (Algeria) in North Africa. I lost a tyre on the transformer raid. We found it difficult picking up the target and I think we must have lost a bit of height and instead of bombing at 1,000 feet I bombed at about 800 feet and we were damaged by the casing of our own bomb. My bomb-aimer was hit on the tip of his nose and it punctured the port tyre. When I landed at Blida I did a great big ground loop, so I had to stay back there for a couple of days before I got another tyre. I took off after the rest and landed at a Ras el Ma [on the Moroccan coastline] to refuel. When I was there waiting to be refuelled a Wing Commander came out and 'cadged' a lift back to England including his three dogs.

And then came the Dortmund-Ems Canal with the tragic loss of five crews out of eight, including Gibson's crew, and that was a real disaster for the squadron and probably the blackest day in the squadron's history really. But then Cheshire arrived and all things changed, and attitude changed and procedures and that sort of thing. A great period I think from then on.

A few weeks after the Dams raid, Gibson was given a new job. Having flown just a single operation with the squadron, Bomber Command believed him to be too valuable to keep on operations. At the age of twenty-four, with a VC, DSO and Bar and DFC and Bar, Gibson was sent on a lecture tour of the United States.

The new commanding officer was George Holden, a highly-decorated bomber pilot who had earned his first DFC in 1941. Taking command of 102 Squadron at Pocklington in October 1942 Holden was awarded a DSO and a Bar to his DFC before the end of his tour. After just two trips with 617 Squadron prior to September 1943, Holden led two operations on successive nights to attack the Dortmund-Ems canal.

Well, the first night eight aircraft went and the conditions reported by the Mosquito reconnoitring over the target were low haze, unsuitable conditions for a low-level attack and so the raid was aborted. That was the night that David Maltby lost his life and those of his crew when he dipped his wing in the sea – an indication of how low we were flying in those days. He must have been pretty low to dip his wing. So the next night they went led by George Holden. It was hazy conditions again but they met unanticipated light flak. The combination meant that they had great difficulty in identifying the target. It was a combination of those factors. We lost five crews.

Holden himself was shot down that night on the way to the target. He was killed along with his crew, one of the most experienced, and most decorated, in Bomber Command. Among those killed that night in Holden's crew were wireless operator Robert Hutchinson, navigator Harlo Taerum, bomb-aimer Fred 'Spam' Spafford and front gunner George Deering, all of whom had been part of Gibson's crew on the

Dams raid. Les Knight, the man who dropped the bomb that breached the Eder Dam, was also killed that night, his crew baling out after the aircraft lost both port engines and suffered a damaged tail.

> I remember Joe [McCarthy] and I sitting in the Ops Room listening to the reports and the fact of losses being reported and we got very downhearted about that. Yeah, I think that knocked the stuffing out the squadron for a little while until eventually Cheshire built up the morale again.

Leonard Cheshire became the new commander of 617 Squadron in September 1943. As a junior pilot officer he joined 102 Squadron flying Armstrong Whitworth Whitleys and was awarded a DSO. His next two tours were at 35 and, then, 76 Squadrons flying Handley Page Halifaxes before he was promoted to Group Captain and made station commander of RAF Marston Moor, a desk job which definitely didn't suit this man of action. Given the opportunity to take over 617 Squadron he took a demotion to Wing Commander and began his fourth tour of the war.

> Despite the fact that I got quite friendly with Cheshire I've always regarded him as a first-class bloke in all respects. He was quiet, rather intense, a deep thinker, and he treated everyone as equals. He never asked us to do anything that he wouldn't do himself. He was always looking for more ways of improving our operations and I don't think he had any fear at all. But of course it's easy to say that when a bloke had done so many operations as he had done. I always say Gibson ordered somebody to do something and Cheshire asked, big difference.
>
> After Cheshire arrived, Mickey Martin was the flight commander. I was promoted to take over B Flight and Mickey had A Flight and that's how it stood until Bob Hay was killed on the Antheor Viaduct. Through a longstanding convention that he had with his crew he ceased operations and then Cheshire took the opportunity to create a three-flight squadron. So he solved the dilemma of what to do with Shannon and McCarthy and Munro. Although I'd already been promoted, he formed a three-flight squadron and promoted David Shannon and Joe McCarthy to be flight commanders, Dave A Flight, me B Flight and Joe McCarthy C Flight

and that was the firm that stayed like that for about another six months.

After the Dams raid no one seemed to know what the squadron was going to do. All that specialist low-level training for just one operation? No operations in June, and just four in July. August was clear as well and then when so many crews were lost on the Dortmund-Ems canal raid it must have seemed that there was no future for 617.

It wasn't until Cheshire took over that we got more *au fait* with what the role was going to be. We were not aware that there'd been any specific designs for our role by Group Headquarters or anything like that. But in the first couple of raids under Cheshire it was felt that the marking of a target by PFF [Pathfinder Force] wasn't quite satisfactory from the squadron's point of view. Cheshire and Micky Martin said, 'right now let's mark them ourselves at low level', and so we were marking targets at low level with Lancasters. I was one of those at the time who felt that the Lanc was a bit too cumbersome for low-level marking; for quick manoeuvrability it wasn't really first class. So Cheshire persuaded Group to give him four Mosquitoes. From then on they marked them from Mosquitoes. Our role then was almost entirely on attacking specific targets on our own without any help from PFF. And so right till the end of the war, the 617 role was attacking specific targets rather than blanket bombing.

Having secured a role the squadron had to find the best ways to mark the targets themselves.

Well in the first place you had to identify it. Somebody would drop flares and then the markers would fly out at about 200 or 300 feet above the target and then dive down and release their markers, coloured bombs, at the last possible moment for accuracy. Cheshire would determine how accurate those markers were and if they were to his satisfaction he'd call me up, this is when I took over as leader of the Lancasters up above, he would call me up and say 'bomb such and such a marker, the markers are OK'. A particular marker might be red or green or blue that night and I had to get the instructions to the other Lancasters to bomb on those directions.

One of the reasons for pinpoint accuracy was they didn't want to create too many casualties among the French population. But another one was to try and do as much damage with the least number of bombs as possible. We were then bombing from 8,000 to 10,000 feet and Cheshire and the other blokes were marking it low level. It was just a question of efficient operations with a small task force rather than blanket bombing, departing from Butch Harris's blanket bombing theories.

Apart from factories we were bombing V-weapons sites. And that was difficult because a lot of them were underground. But I think on the whole the policy of the low-level marking techniques was so successful that Cochrane, the AOC of 5 Group, decided we'd adopt the same method for 5 Group as a whole. So that was the stage when he brought 619 and 83 squadrons back from Pathfinder Force to 5 Group and seconded them to Woodhall Spa where they were to be instructed in the techniques that Cheshire had evolved. We had two operations, one of which didn't prove particularly satisfactory. Weather conditions were not too good. PFF squadron didn't drop the flares very accurately and there was interference from one of the PFF squadron flight crew who left his mike on. All his chatter was being broadcast to all and sundry and that of course restricted Cheshire being able to communicate with me and others from his marking force. So that was not particularly successful but two nights later we went to Munich and that was a highly successful raid. Cheshire marked that target in conjunction with Dave Shannon and Gerry Fawke. That was very successful and was the last 617 carried out in conjunction with the main bomber force. I think we had created a standard that was recognised as being pretty efficient. We had developed the use of the SABS bombing sight to pretty high standard of accuracy and I think that was recognised by the powers-that-be for that reason. I'm not sure as to the background as to whether Butch Harris requested 5 Group or whether Sir Ralph Cochrane was asked by the Air Ministry to undertake the D Day operation. But it would have been due to the fact that by that time 617 had built up a reputation for efficiency and accuracy.

The New Year of 1944 seemed to be the turning point for the squadron. Losses dropped, Cheshire's new target-marking system was proving successful and the squadron started a campaign of attacks on special targets such as V-1 sites, aero engine factories, railway yards and signals depots, most contributing to the build-up for the Normandy invasion.

By the end of April 1944 Les Munro had flown twenty-seven operations with 617 Squadron.

After the Munich raid we were told that we'd been taken off operations to train for another specific operation and that upset a lot of the crews considerably. Those that had been with us for a long time enjoyed operating. So we trained up at Flamborough Head for this operation and it was purely a navigational exercise doing circuits. At the end of the day it turned out to be the Operation TAXABLE.

Operation TAXABLE was part of the radar countermeasures deception plan to keep the Germans guessing where the invasion would come. Flown on the night of 5/6 June 1944, the squadron simulated a 'ghost' convoy approaching Cap d'Antifer to the east of the actual landing area. It required absolutely accurate timing from the crews involved with an error of no more than four seconds being allowed for each manoeuvre.

We were briefed that D Day was on. We took off about eleven o'clock, that was the first we knew that D Day was on and I suppose we had a great deal of satisfaction in knowing that we played a part in the D Day operation. It was a spoof raid and involved two waves of eight aircraft each, the first wave flying for two hours, the second wave taking over for another two hours. It involved oblong circuits starting from a predetermined distance from the English coast and flying in a straight line to the French coast for two minutes thirty seconds, doing a 180-degree turn to port, returning on the parallel course to the first degree for two minutes ten seconds and then doing another turn to port for a distance of twenty seconds. The outward and return legs were both carried out by all eight aircraft, advancing towards the French coast at eight knots. All the time we're doing these circuits the crew in the back of the aircraft were dropping aluminium tin foil or 'Window' as we used to call it in increasing size as we went toward the French coast, decreasing as we came back, no tin foil being dropped on the turns. So we had a whole pattern of this tin foil over a sixteen-mile front creating an illusion of a large armada on the German radar systems. Leonard Cheshire was my second pilot on that operation because he had no longer had a Lancaster crew, just his navigator, so I carried thirteen 'bods' that day including Cheshire and me. Most of the planes had fourteen, two crews – two lots of seven, doubled up because of the boring and repetitive nature of the actions we had to do, particularly the blokes in the rear where they were funnelling the 'Window' down the chute. After an hour Cheshire took over from me. The navigators really had two separate jobs to do; one navigator was directing the courses whereas the second navigator was operating the time system: starting dropping the 'Window' and stopping – red and green lights when to stop when to start. Also they were advising when to upgrade the size of the 'Window' the closer we got to the French coast. On the whole I think it created sufficient disquiet in the German minds to postpone reinforcements over the Normandy front and it may just have made only two or three hours difference but it made enough difference to help.

Another illustration of the timing involved came after two hours. The second wave came on and each individual aircraft came over the top of the aircraft it was going to replace at 500 feet above just at the same time as the aircraft from the first flight was starting the last circuit and both aircraft flew the circuit together and at the end of the return leg, the aircraft from the first wave took off home and the replacing aircraft dropped down 500 feet to the same level as the first. We only had ninety seconds in which to complete that manoeuvre. Another indication of the timing exact timing required.

I will say today this is probably one of the most important operations we had to carry out during my time on squadron, mainly because of the exact nature we had to fly. Airspeed, course, rate of turn, everything had to be exact.

Barnes Wallis had followed up his invention of the bouncing bomb with that of an 'earthquake' bomb, designed to penetrate the ground near a target and explode underneath. Delay fuses meant that it could be set to explode anywhere from thirty seconds to thirty minutes later. 617 Squadron used it to great effect after D Day, their first operation using the bomb being an attack on a tunnel near Saumur in western France, some 200 kilometres south of the invasion area. The plan was to destroy the tunnel, preventing German Panzer reinforcements reaching Normandy.

On 8 June we bombed the Saumur Tunnel with Tallboys for the first time. That was that was quite an experience for me. Cheshire and I had discovered Tallboys arriving on the squadron a few days prior to that and we thought 'Hello, this is going to be good' because we'd been using ordinary 12,000-pounder 'Blockbusters' for most of my operations other than when 500 or 1,000-pounders were required. The aiming point was the mouth of the tunnel but this bomb landed way up the hill on the line of the railway track and penetrated right down before exploding down at railway level. It certainly blocked the line there at that vital time when reinforcements were being rushed by the Germans up to the front.

And then a few days later we hit the submarine pens at le Havre and then a night later Boulogne and I had the privilege of leading the squadron in the daylight on that raid. That was the first time the squadron had operated in daylight. Then, for some reason, we went in formation to le Havre with a fighter escort which we couldn't see as they were way above us and then on Boulogne on the next night. The next day we went singly again in daylight and the result of those two operations was that we destroyed 133 E-boats and made massive damage to the submarine pens. Those were the Tallboys. The Tallboy was probably the most efficient and aerodynamically perfect bomb that you could have got. It was a smaller version of Barnes Wallis's original Grand Slam bomb which he thought might be needed to destroy the dams.

I found that the fact that we had 12,000 pounds slung underneath us didn't make a great deal of difference. Certainly you had the feeling that you were carrying more weight and as a consequence you could sense that you were requiring a bit more power. When you released the Tallboy you had an immediate reaction as far as height was concerned.

The squadron was pretty efficient at using SABS and the powers-that-be impressed on us the value of these bombs, that you've got to make every one count. So it was impressed on the crews, don't waste these things.

[SABS] stood for Stabilised Automatic Bomb Sight. It was much more accurate used at high level than the existing bomb-sight and, I think, used in conjunction with the Tallboy, it was very effective.

We used to train consistently at high level using the bomb-sight but only with a seven-and-a-half-pound practice bomb. I think on the whole the crews on the squadron became quite proficient in the use of the bomb-sight.

I think we were given certain targets because of our ability to mark as a small accurate force and very seldom did we fail. Only adverse weather conditions, when the visual condition was such that you couldn't identify the targets. I think it was St Étienne where we weren't too successful that night. We went there and it was very difficult to pick up the target because of ground haze. But the bulk, I'd say over ninety per cent, of our targets we caused considerable damage if not complete damage.

On 6 July 617 Squadron attacked construction works near Mimoy-ecques, some eight kilometres from the French coast near Cap Gris Nez. The Germans were building a site for their V-3 supergun which was to be used to bombard London. Huge 400-foot-long barrels were sunk into massive underground tunnels with just the end of the barrels showing above ground. It was a very difficult target to attack with so little showing above ground. Using Tallboys the squadron scored one direct hit and some near misses which brought down the tunnel roof and damaged the barrels putting the site completely out of commission.

We had bombed one of the V-weapons sites and I think it was the next day or two days later that Sir Ralph Cochrane came down and informed Cheshire, Dave Shannon, McCarthy and myself that he was taking us off operations. It was just like that. Most upsetting for me because I was a couple short of sixty operations and I had my sights set on sixty. I think you could say that as far as Dave Shannon and McCarthy were concerned they were both disappointed they were taken off operations. But I suppose you look back in hindsight it was probably wise, we had to finish sometime. But in my case I would've like to have done another couple. I'm not sure whether Cochrane had advised Shannon or McCarthy what their future was but he certainly called me out and he said 'I want you to take over the 1690 Bomber Defence Training Flight,' he said, 'I'm not altogether happy with the results there'. So he wanted me to take over that and so I had to change from four engines to one engine, quite an experience.

Munro stayed flying Hurricanes at 1690 BDTF until July 1945. After the war he left the service and returned to his native New Zealand. He worked on land valuation for the resettlement of ex-servicemen, became a farmer and got involved with local politics. His list of decorations got ever longer. He was awarded the DSO and DFC during the war, was appointed Companion of the Queen's Service Order in 1991 and Companion of the New Zealand Order of Merit in 1997.

He continues to live in New Zealand and, at the time of writing, is one of just three survivors of the legendary Dams raid.

Squadron Leader Les Munro – Operations at 617 Squadron

- 16/17 May 1943 – Sorpe Dam – Hit by flak over Holland and returned to Scampton with the bomb still on board. The target was hit by two bombs dropped by other crews but was not breached.
- 15 July 1943 – San Polo D'enza – Electrical transformer station. Target partially obscured by mist and was not destroyed. The twelve Lancasters of 617 Squadron bombed and then flew on to North Africa, landing safely at Blida.
- 24 July 1943 – Leghorn [Livorno] – Dock and harbour installations. Bombing was carried out on the return journey from North Africa. Again mist obscured the target and bombs were dropped on the estimated position of the marshalling yards.
- 29 July 1943 – Genoa – NICKEL raid dropping leaflets on Italian cities. Again the aircraft were flown on to Blida and returned between 1 and 8 August.
- 16 September 1943 – Antheor Viaduct – Attack on the viaduct carrying the railway line along the south coast of France near Cannes. Results were not seen due to delayed fuses in the bombs but no actual hits were registered.
- 11 November 1943 – Antheor Viaduct – First operation with the new SABS bomb-sight. 12,000lb bombs dropped but no hits were registered. Again the aircraft landed at Blida, returning to Scampton on 18 November.
- 16 December 1943 – Special target – Flixecourt flying-bomb site near Abbeville. Accurate bombing but dropped on misdirected markers. Target not destroyed.
- 20 December 1943 – Liege – Armament works. Mission abandoned as markers could not be seen below cloud.

- 22 December 1943 – Special target – Flying-bomb site. Mission abandoned again.
- 30 December 1943 – Special target – Flixecourt flying-bomb site. Again accurate bombing but dropped on misdirected markers. Target not destroyed.
- 4 January 1944 – Special target – Pas de Calais flying-bomb site. Target attacked successfully and heavily damaged.
- 21 January 1944 – Special target – Flying-bomb site. Target attacked successfully.
- 25 January 1944 – Special target – Flying-bomb site. Target attacked successfully.
- 12 February 1944 – Antheor Viaduct. Target attacked for the third time but only near misses obtained.
- 2 March 1944 – Albert – Aircraft factory. Very successful operation with the factory being virtually destroyed.
- 4 March 1944 – St Étienne – la Ricamerie needle-bearing factory. Operation abandoned as target was not located due to cloud.
- 10 March 1944 – St Étienne – la Ricamerie needle-bearing factory. Operation only partially successful as target only slightly damaged. Many of the markers bounced off the factory.
- 15 March 1944 – Woippy – Aero-engine factory. Operation abandoned as target obscured by cloud.
- 16 March 1944 – Clermont-Ferrand – Michelin tyre factory. Very successful precision raid. Leonard Cheshire flew over the factory three times to warn French workers. Target destroyed.
- 18 March 1944 – Bergerac – Explosives factory. Factory completely destroyed.
- 20 March 1944 – Angouleme – Explosives factory. Target completely destroyed.
- 5 April 1944 – Toulouse – Bréguet/Latécoère aircraft factories. Squadron acted as markers for the Main Force. The first low-level Mosquito marking flight of the war. Target destroyed.
- 10 April 1944 – St Cyr – Signals depot. Very successful operation. Target destroyed.
- 18 April 1944 – Juvisy – Marshalling yards. 617 Squadron acted as markers for 5 Group. Target destroyed.
- 20 April 1944 – la Chapelle – Railway yards in the north area of Paris. Target heavily bombed. It was the first test for the new 5 Group marking method using 617 Squadron plus further 5 Group Pathfinder squadrons. Very successful operation.

- 22 April 1944 – Brunswick – First use of 5 Group's marking method over a German city. Cloud hindered the bombing of the target.
- 24 April 1944 – Munich – 617 Squadron again provided part of the marking force for Main Force. Bombing was accurate and the operation successful.
- 5 June 1944 – Operation TAXABLE – 617 Squadron flew very accurate runs towards the French coast dropping 'Window' to simulate an allied convoy approaching. Totally successful, the operation helped to keep German forces away from the real invasion area.
- 8 June 1944 – Saumur – Railway tunnel. The first use of the Tallboy 12,000lb 'earthquake' bomb. Target destroyed, stopping many German reserves being brought to the Normandy front by rail.
- 14 June 1944 – le Havre – E-boat pens. Carried out in daylight, the raid proved that the Tallboy bombs could penetrate the massively thick concrete shelters which the Germans thought to be bombproof.
- 15 June 1944 – Boulogne – E-boat pens. Not as successful as the previous night's raid as many of the aircraft brought back their bombs but still much damage was caused.
- 22 June 1944 – Wizernes – V-2 weapons site. Recalled when the target could not be found due to cloud.
- 24 June 1944 – Wizernes – V-2 weapons site. This time the squadron found and bombed the target, a storage facility being built for V-2 rockets. The site was put out of use.
- 25 June 1944 – Siracourt – Flying-bomb storage facility. Target successfully attacked. 617 Squadron CO marked the target using a Mustang he had never flown before.
- 6 July 1944 – Mimoyecques – V-3 weapons site. The site was put out of use.

Les Munro was posted from the squadron on 13 July 1944 to 1690 Bomber Defence Training Flight.

Chapter 2

Warrant Officer Grant McDonald

Grant McDonald was born in Grand Forks, some 310 miles east of Vancouver, British Columbia, in 1921, second youngest of a family of seven. After school he wanted to join the Royal Canadian Air Force but as they were not recruiting at that time he joined the Canadian Army instead.

> When I joined up I came out of school and the same day, 24 June 1940, I joined the Army. I joined the Seaforth Highlanders [of Canada]. I stayed with them for about nine months and I was transferred to the Calgary Tank Regiment and I made an application to join the Air Force and was accepted. In order to go you had to be discharged for that purpose, not re-enlist in the Air Force. So that was how I got my start there.

Grant's initial training was with 21 Elementary Flying Training School at Chatham, New Brunswick, where he flew in Fleet Finches. These were Canadian two-seat biplane trainers, built by Fleet Aircraft of Fort Erie in Ontario. Grant didn't make it as a pilot, so he was sent on an air gunners' course, flying in Fairey Battles. On completion of this course Grant travelled to the UK on the MS *Batory*, a converted Polish ocean liner which was used as a troop transport and hospital ship and, on one occasion in 1940, to transport much of the UK's gold reserves to Canada. Landing at Greenock he travelled by train to the other end of the country, the Reception Centre at Bournemouth on the south coast of Britain.

> After leaving the reception centre I was sent to a gunnery course again – a refresher gunnery course [at Castle Kennedy near Stranraer in Scotland] – and then to 19 OTU at Kinloss. There the crew was formed, a crew of five. Ken Brown, I had the choice of getting in with members of his crew and that's how I came about

to be part of it. I always got along alright with him and didn't seem to have any problems.

Ken Brown was also Canadian, born in 1920 in Moose Jaw, Saskatchewan.

> The navigator, Dudley Heal, was an older chap, he was five years older than I was. He was very good, had very good ratings from when he became a navigator. I think he was one of the more important members of the crew. The wireless operator, Harry Hewstone, was also older than we were. And the bomb-aimer, by the name of Stefan Oancia, was a very bright chap. We knew we had no problems with him.
>
> Actually we seemed to work very well together. Ken Brown kept in contact with you. He would constantly call me on the intercom and reassure me that everything was alright. He did that on all operations.

During his training in the UK Grant McDonald had been flying in Armstrong Whitworth Whitley Mk Vs and, after completing their time at OTU, the crew was posted to fly anti-submarine patrols from St Eval in Cornwall.

> After OTU had finished we went down to St Eval, and they had a shortage of anti-submarine aircraft at that time and so, instead of going to a conversion unit at that time where we should have gone, we were sent down there to go on Whitleys and do sweeps in the Bay of Biscay. It was November and when you left it was dark in the morning. Dudley the navigator was always saying, 'That's Bishop's Rock, have a good look at it because you're not going to see it for a while,' Those sweeps were eight, nine, ten hours before you got back. You had to be careful all that time because you had to keep below the level of cloud maybe at 1,000 or 1,200 feet over the water in the daytime, you were in and out of it. On one particular sweep a bunch of tracer came up at us, firing at us. It was a US convoy going to North Africa. They opened fire before we had a chance to fire the colours of the day. Had they seen that, they would have stopped firing. So you had to be on the watch at all times, you never got bored.

After just a few patrols they were sent to a Lancaster heavy conversion unit at Wigsley, ten miles from Lincoln and finally met up with their last two crew members. In February 1943 they received a posting to 44 Squadron at Waddington.

> I think our first operation as a crew was to Munich and we somehow got a little off track going. We were quite a bit north of the city when we got there. We could see the searchlights and the bombing going on so we headed to it. As we were late we got a full packet that night, then all the way on the return from Augsburg. By that time we'd corkscrewed and dived and everything and we were down to 6,000 feet. That was our first experience together as a crew.

As rear gunner Grant was the eyes of the crew at the back of the aircraft.

> You scan the area that you can. I kept going all the time whether it was seven or eight hours, I never stopped. I paid special attention to the quarters particularly to the dark side of the sky. Both those quarters were the place you had to keep an eye on and up and down, obviously. You would report anything unusual to the pilot.
>
> I just saw one night-fighter one night. He came by but he didn't turn in. He just flew right by. I guess he didn't pick us up and he just went right across the sky.
>
> You were in contact with the pilot on the intercom. Ken kept on at you all the time to make sure because something like this could've happened. I was more concerned all the time with 'how am I going to get out of here?' in case I had to get out. You had to get your 'chute first, as it was outside, and a lot of times it was on the floor, it had fallen out of the rack on the wall and down on the floor. And [you had to decide] whether you were going to fall out backwards or if you had time to get to the door? If you got out the door there was always the possibility that you were going to get hit by the tailplane. So that was constantly on your mind: 'How you were going to escape if you had to get out in a hurry?'
>
> It was very cold but I had an electrically-heated suit. It was like a coverall that you plugged into the system and all you had to wear then was the white sweater and I wore Irvin pants. It was

alright although I couldn't get into the turret with that big Irvin jacket on.

The guns would go unserviceable sometimes. The guns in the rear turret were fed up through the floor; the trays were on the sides of the fuselage. I don't know how many rounds were in them, but the section where they came up and went into the gun was where your jams usually took place. I looked after them pretty good. I used to lubricate them. Two armourers told me one day when I was cleaning them up and pulling them through that nobody else did that. I was all on my own on that.

Eventually most crews did at least one trip to Berlin, the German capital, which was considered one of the toughest targets. It was deep into Germany and was one of the longest flights to and from a target. It was heavily defended, not just because it was the capital but because it was vital to German war production. Grant and his crew did their only trip to Berlin in March 1943.

We just did one Berlin. That was a fiasco because I had a bit of a cold. I was breathing through my mouth and my oxygen tube froze. By the time we got to the target Ken was doing his usual, calling at me. I was answering him but he couldn't hear me. So we got there, north of the city, and got the bombing in and the wireless operator came back, opened up and pulled me back out of the turret. In doing so he broke the corrugated hose that went from the oxygen distribution to your mask. He broke that off because I still had it on my face. So he got me the emergency, we had an emergency bottle with a mask, and got me on that and got me back. The only result was that I had a very bad headache for two days. That was our trip to Berlin, just the one.

After just a month with 44 Squadron Ken Brown and his crew were posted to the newly forming 617 Squadron at Scampton.

We were on 44 Squadron and why we were selected I would not know. We were just chosen I guess, to fill the roster for crews going to 617. We worked very well. If you didn't I don't think you would be there very long. The Wing Commander would have seen to that. You would have been pushed back probably to your old squadron that you came from.

Ken Brown was a flight sergeant at this time and the rest of his crew were all sergeants or flight sergeants as well. So not only did most of the crew not have any contact with the squadron commander, Wing Commander Guy Gibson, but many had very little to do with any officers at all.

> You didn't have any association with the officers whatsoever. And they had their own mess and so you never contacted Gibson. The only time I saw him would be in the briefing both for the practice and the actual raid, itself. That was the only time you had any contact with Gibson. I found one of the men who isn't known very much was Melvin Young. He was very good, very good organiser and an older chap, I found him very good. He was our flight commander.

Melvin Young had been nicknamed 'Dinghy' because he had been shot down twice before on raids and in both cases had survived with his crew in rubber dinghies. The first time, in October 1940, he ditched his Whitley and the whole crew survived. He was to ditch again before the end of his tour after which he was posted to 104 Squadron flying Wellingtons in the Middle East. He was awarded two DFCs and was a natural choice as a flight commander for this new squadron.

Grant McDonald particularly remembered the security imposed on all squadron personnel.

> All the telephone lines were tapped at base. On one occasion we were all called in and there had been a phone call made and Guy Gibson got up and actually read the telephone call out that this chap made, which was very embarrassing for him because he had to listen to it. It was just an example of the things you don't do. It was embarrassing for the chap. His girlfriend, I think, lived in Lincoln and this was this conversation with his girlfriend.

Training was vital in the squadron as, not only were they a new squadron with crews who had spent very little time together, their operation was to involve very low-level and accurate flying.

> You had to go on them all; the entire crew took part in them. We did some low-level bombing exercises down on the Wash and

they were pretty tricky to get down to the sixty foot level, just to drop these smaller practice bombs.

It was a bomb that was hydrostatically fused so that by the time it dropped to the depth it was supposed to be at, you'd gone by. I could see the explosion and it was well clear by that time. It was quite large.

We spent a lot of time crossing rivers and that sort of thing where there were bridges. That seemed to stick out more than flying across that part of England which is quite level. I don't recall any real close calls we had during the training.

Like every other crewman Grant was completely unaware of their target.

We were never told a thing about what the target was going to be, preparing the way we did with the low-level flying and the low-level bombing practices. We had no idea. We were forever guessing but we had no idea that it would be the dams. The rumour went round that it would be on some type of shipping, perhaps a battleship or else some of the submarine bases in and around the Normandy coast. They were also mentioned. But it was never mentioned about the dams.

As I was only a gunner, we didn't know. I believe the pilots and navigators knew the day before or something like that but we didn't know. I didn't know until the main briefing, until we walked into the briefing room and saw the actual models of the dams. Our regular gunner went on sick parade that morning so we had to use another gunner, Daniel Allatson, from a crew that didn't go. I didn't know him so we put him in the front turret.

I thought that if this was going to be the type of raid it was, a low-level raid, there would possibly be little interference from fighters so you had to more or less concentrate on what was on the ground, what could you do, if there was anything, with ground turrets? There wasn't much else that you could do.

The low-level flying part of it, I felt, would be rather dangerous, particularly on a moonlit night. Even though if it's a moonlight night, there are still a lot of shadows to go through. That was the only part that concerned me: the getting there and once you got there to get out of there to get home, to get back to base.

Apparently they had the positions of the flak and searchlights pretty well known. They were made known to the pilot and navigator and we were told not to wander off track.

Ken Brown flew AJ-F, F for Freddie, on the dams raid of 16/17 May 1943. They were part of a mobile reserve given the job of attacking a secondary target but each prepared to divert to attack one of the main dams, the Möhne or Eder. Taking off three hours after the first and second waves, the five aircraft all had different adventures. The aircraft of Warner Ottley was shot down on the way to his target, the Lister dam. One crew member survived. Similarly Lewis Burpee's aircraft was shot down, but with no survivors. Bill Townsend attacked the Bever Dam, mistaking it for his actual target, the Ennerpe Dam. Cyril Anderson arrived late at the Sorpe dam and, with the lake now covered in mist, aborted his attack and brought his bomb home to base.

Ken Brown and his crew, however, had an adventure all of their own.

I had an opportunity to shoot up a couple of trains that were coming by. They were in the dark side of the sky from the moon so I don't suppose it did much damage.

We took the same route as the other nine aircraft that left earlier. They went in formation, but we went singly. We went above the Scheldt and came in between Eindhoven and the Luftwaffe base at Gilze-Rijen and carried on to Rees and crossed the Rhine. We then turned more or less south eastwards, I guess more or less to the dams, and we went directly to the Sorpe. It was very bad between Eindhoven and the German base and an aircraft went down very close to us. We were caught in the same anti-aircraft fire, it was very intense, very intense – and the searchlights. We were so low that that the trees were silhouetted against the searchlights. That's how low we were. We must have been at 60 feet, maybe even lower, which saved us. The aircraft that went down exploded the bomb. It wasn't that far [away] and, of course, we were caught in the same fire, although they were [behind] us. We got through that alright, got to Rees and it was quiet there. After that the fire was a little more distant. There was anti-aircraft fire, a lot of anti-aircraft fire, but it was more distant and we saw another aircraft go down. He was off track. He had got over Hamm, I think, and we saw him go down. We didn't know who these aircraft were they were but both of them were from our flight.

I guess if we'd gone higher we'd have had to get down to put that bomb away, to drop that bomb. They felt that with proper navigation keeping on track and having known where these bases were they could possibly get through them. But I always thought afterwards that the most difficult part of the whole operation was getting there and getting home again. Because actually when you think of it there was only one aircraft lost at that moment [of attack]; John Hopgood's aircraft was shot down. The rest were killed on the way in or the way out. So it was it was new for Bomber Command to choose this type of low-level approach.

Brown's aircraft arrived over the Sorpe Dam at about 3.00am. There were no defences on the dam but that didn't make the attack any easier.

It took several runs, I don't recall how many, but it took several runs. And one thing I'd like to bring out is that recently they've come out with this story that we approached the thing from the right angle, but that is not right. We came parallel with the wall of the dam on the reservoir side, just inside the reservoir side parallel to the wall.

He [Ken Brown] was trying to get it right and in line with the wall. The approach, I believe, came rather down over a hill and then down towards the dam. But he just couldn't seem to get it right.

I had a very good view. There was a bit of fog earlier but it rolled back like fog does and it rolled back like cloud to form a wall more or less. It was quite clear when we went. But that was earlier and probably one of the reasons for the runs, until this fog cleared. It cleared on the reservoir side, on the water side.

Eventually, after eight runs at the dam, Brown dropped incendiary bombs in the woods at either end. These both illuminated the target and helped to clear the fog. One more run was made and the bomb was dropped.

It [the bomb] bounced a little bit; it bounced a couple of times. It didn't go straight in. It bounced a couple of times before it sank.

We were well round on our circuit to get away when the bomb went and I saw this huge wall of water come up. But you couldn't actually tell if there was any damage. You knew the wall wasn't broken but you could see far enough back that there was some crumbling just on the surface. And that was it. As a matter of fact I was telling Brown as he was making these circuits, I said, 'Let's get out of here. Get out of here as quickly as you can,' because you knew what it was like coming in and [what] you'd got to face going back out again. But it didn't seem to bother him very much as he continued making these circuits until he got it right.

Brown bombed at 3.14am but, instead of going straight home, he flew to see what damage had been done to the primary target, the Möhne Dam.

We went over to the Möhne Dam but we kept our distance from it because the guns were still firing from there. We returned the fire but it was not much use at that distance with 303s. As we went home there was light flak along the way. But we crossed the Zuiderzee and came into that part of Northern Holland called Den Helder. As soon as we hit the shore of the land up it came, a terrific amount of anti-aircraft fire and searchlights. Ken got down as low as he could but we got hit and hit bad. I thought, 'Well, it's all over' but he got down low enough to get it out on the other side and head back to base. It was in much the same area where they got Melvin Young on his way out. He was not far, caught in the same anti-aircraft fire. It was very, very bad.

Young was shot down by flak and his aircraft crashed into the sea. This time, however, he did not get out. He and his crew were killed and their bodies washed up on the Dutch shore some days later.

We were blinded by the searchlights. The best you could do was fire away at both the guns and the searchlights. But it reached the point where you knew that they had you and you didn't know whether you were doing any good or not.

At one point the aircraft was holed by a flak burst and riddled with shrapnel. Ken Brown was flying the aircraft at fifty feet and still the flak was hitting them. So he reduced height again and now the guns had to fire downwards to register hits on the aircraft. But despite all the flak holes and apparent damage the aircraft kept on flying.

There was nothing, no damage done. It was very fortunate. Another yard and it could have hit the cockpit quite easily.

The sky is a kind of a light grey at that time of the morning before it becomes daylight. It's kind of an eerie feeling when the sky is like that as you know that it's not long until daylight. Everything had been so calm when we crossed the Zuider Zee. The water was calm and all of sudden, as soon as we hit the land, we got hit. I remember the bomb-aimer made the comment that it was a miracle that we survived that last attack.

Brown landed his aircraft at 5.30am, the last but one to arrive back at Scampton, beating Bill Townsend by almost forty-five minutes.

What got me most was the next morning when you saw the lorries going to the huts and taking all the effects of all the people. We didn't know then just how many didn't come back because we went to lie down for a bit of rest. And that hit you then that so many weren't coming back. I don't think they had any idea it would be that many.

Normally you would probably have gone again maybe a night or two afterwards if you were on ordinary operations. We didn't and they gave us a bit of leave and but it takes a while to wear off. All these people were missing, faces you'd seen at teatime were not there anymore.

The squadron reassembled after leave, new faces arrived and training restarted.

There was more training all the time, trying something a little different. A lot of bombing practice, cross-countries. It must have been July before we went on a shuttle trip to Italy and went on to Algeria and stayed there for five days and bombed Italy coming back again.

We did the Antheor Viaduct. That was a long trip – shuttle. A lot of them were these flying-bomb sites in France which were short trips.

The squadron had not undertaken a trip for almost two months after the dams raid when they restarted operations on 15 July 1943. For Grant McDonald this was an attack on an electrical transformer station north of Genoa in northern Italy, followed by a landing in North Africa. Ten days later they took off, bombed the docks at Leghorn, otherwise known as Livorno, in Italy and landed back at base without loss. Neither raid was very successful, due to haze over the targets, and it would be another few weeks before the next operation.

And then came the fateful two trips to the Dortmund-Ems Canal.

We didn't have to go on that. They gave it to the crews who had illness and were unable to go to the Dams operation, they let them go, also including the new wing commander, George Holden, we lost him that night. It was rather a disaster really. That put an end to the low-level bombing.

I think eight or nine of them went the first night. A reconnaissance aircraft had been sent and the weather was bad over the target. So, they were recalled. And they lost an aircraft, Maltby's aircraft in the North Sea, nobody knows what happened. And they went again the next night. There were reports that some got too high and they didn't keep down enough.

It shook everybody up for a while when that happened. To lose five of the eight in one night and one the night before. Unbelievable really.

The disasters of the Dortmund-Ems Canal trips left just six of the original nineteen Dambusters' crews flying with the Squadron. Les Munro, Dave Shannon and Joe McCarthy became the new flight commanders under Cheshire and carried on with 617 until July 1944. Geoff Rice was shot down on a trip to the Antheor Viaduct in southern France on 20 December 1943, hidden by the Resistance for six months, but eventually captured. He spent the rest of the war as a PoW. Mick Martin became temporary commanding officer of 617 Squadron after the death of George Holden and until Leonard Cheshire arrived. He then carried on with the squadron until February 1944 when his bomb-aimer, Bob Hay, was killed on a trip to bomb the Antheor Viaduct. This was to be his last operation with the squadron.

This operation was also to be the last for Ken Brown and his crew. Ken went on a course and finally left the squadron in May 1944. Grant McDonald left on 26 March and was posted as an instructor to

29 OTU at Bruntingthorpe. In total he had done twenty-seven operations including the Coastal Command sweeps.

> They gave him [Ken Brown] the choice I believe, whether he wanted to stay on but I went, I didn't stay. I would have had to pick up with a new crew. And we'd been there quite a while, although we didn't get that many operations in, we'd been there a long time. But that wasn't our fault.

Grant went back to Canada at the end of the war and was demobbed. He then joined the Canadian Customs Service in Vancouver. He had always looked at the modern day interest surrounding 617 Squadron's wartime exploits and, in particular, the dams raid with some surprise, but had his own view on where the credit should lie.

> It is bit different when you realise that we're still much in the forefront of people's minds. I think myself that what really doesn't get mentioned that much is Barnes Wallis, for his participation in bringing the Dams raid about. I don't think he was ever given enough credit because he made it all possible.

Grant took part in many of the celebrations and commemorations with an ever dwindling group of Dambusters until his death in May 2012.

Warrant Officer Grant McDonald – Operations at 617 Squadron

- 16/17 May 1943 – Sorpe Dam – Ken Brown's crew was the second and last to bomb the Sorpe Dam. Mine dropped accurately but dam not breached.
- 15 July 1943 – Aquata Scrivia – Electrical transformer station near Genoa. Target partially obscured by mist and was not destroyed. The twelve Lancasters of 617 Squadron bombed and then flew on to North Africa, landing safely at Blida.
- 24 July 1943 – Leghorn [Livorno] – Dock and harbour installations. Bombing was carried out on the return journey from North Africa. Again mist obscured the target and bombs were dropped on the estimated position of the marshalling yards.
- 16 September 1943 – Antheor Viaduct – Attack on the viaduct carrying the railway line along the south coast of France near Cannes. Results were not seen due to delayed fuses in the bombs but no actual hits were registered.

- 11 November 1943 – Antheor Viaduct – First operation with the new SABS bomb sight. 12,000lb bombs dropped but no hits were registered. Again the aircraft landed at Blida, returning to Scampton on 18 November.
- 16 December 1943 – Special target – Flixecourt flying-bomb site near Abbeville. Accurate bombing but dropped on misdirected markers. Target not destroyed.
- 22 December 1943 – Special target – Flying-bomb site. Mission abandoned.
- 30 December 1943 – Special target – Flixecourt flying-bomb site. Accurate bombing but dropped on misdirected markers. Target not destroyed.
- 4 January 1944 – Special Target – Pas de Calais flying-bomb site. Target attacked successfully and heavily damaged.
- 21 January 1944 – Special Target – Flying-bomb site. Target attacked successfully.
- 8 February 1944 – Limoges – Gnome-Rhône aero-engine factory. The first official operation where 617 Squadron marked its own target. After three low-level passes by Leonard Cheshire to ensure French workers got out, the factory suffered massive damage with hardly any French casualties.
- 12 February 1944 – Antheor Viaduct – Near misses but viaduct hardly damaged.

Grant McDonald was posted to 29 OTU on 26 March 1944.

Chapter 3

Pilot Officer George 'Johnny' Johnson

George 'Johnny' Johnson was born in 1921 in the small village of Hameringham, just to the south east of Horncastle in Lincolnshire. Within a few miles of his birthplace are locations with names that have been immortalised by the daring deeds undertaken by Bomber Command in the Second World War. Many of these were to become important to Johnny during his wartime career. Just to the west is Woodhall Spa where Johnny would spend his first tour with 97 Squadron and, later on, most of his time with 617 Squadron. To the south-east are the ranges at Wainfleet where countless hours would be spent practising his chosen RAF trade of bomb-aimer. And a few miles to the north-west is Scampton, legendary home of the Dambusters, from where Johnny, as one of them, would set out on perhaps his finest hour in May 1943.

I joined the RAF in November 1940. I didn't feel that I had the capability or co-ordination to be a pilot so I just volunteered for aircrew but the selection committee thought differently and they recommended me for pilot training. It took a long time to get into the training system and eventually I got through to Babbacombe for the No.1 Aircrew Reception Centre, Newquay, for Initial Training Wing and then up to Wilmslow to wait for a ship out to Canada to go out to America for pilot training.

Before the Japanese attack on the US Navy's Pacific Fleet at Pearl Harbor in December 1941 America was quietly providing training for British aircrew. It was called the Arnold scheme and the British crews had to travel to Canada dressed in civilian clothes before crossing over to the United States.

When I got out to America there were two systems of pilot training in America at that time. We had our own people out there. They called it the BFTS, the British Flying Training School. Some went to those and others went to the [US] Army Air Corps for training. I got the Army Air Corps down in Arcadia in Florida, and I began to get the distinct 'non-feeling' about the Army Air Corps. I thought their discipline was petty. I thought their marching was so bloody sloppy that it was terrible and, by and large, I just didn't like the Army Air Corps. But the flying instructors were civilians. I didn't blame them at all for the fact that I didn't make the grade because I didn't really think I would ever do it.

The training in Arcadia was carried out by a private flying school. Embry-Riddle was an aircraft dealership and airmail carrier which opened a school of aviation in 1941. The airfields had been used for training airmen during and after the First World War but for the next war it was both Army Air Corps and RAF airmen who trained there. However, No. 5 BFTS for the RAF opened in September 1941. Over the next four years more than a thousand British airmen would receive their wings there.

We went on from Arcadia up to Maxwell Field in Montgomery, Alabama, to wait, then waited in Canada for a ship to get us back to England. I joined in November 1940, we got back to England in January of 1942 and I was no nearer the aircrew war than I had wanted to be in the first place so I thought: which is the quickest course? And the quickest course, of course, was gunnery. So I volunteered for gunnery training and it was back through the old routine, back to the selection committee and so on. I remember the president at the selection board said to me, 'I think you'd be afraid to be a gunner, Johnson.' I said, 'I don't think so, Sir. If I was I wouldn't have volunteered in the first place.' And that was the end of that conversation.

So, I went, I did my gunnery training, and for some unknown reason I wasn't posted to an Operational Training Unit, I was posted direct to 97 Squadron as a spare gunner which meant that I flew with any crew that hadn't got a rear gunner or a mid-upper gunner. It wasn't entirely the best situation to be in but I spent quite a lot of that time flying with one of the flight commanders' crews.

So Johnny's introduction to operational flying was as a gunner for one of the squadron's most senior pilots, Squadron Leader Coton, already a veteran of two attacks on the mighty German battleship, *Tirpitz*. With Coton as pilot Johnny flew his first operation to Gdynia [now Gdansk], the Polish seaport which had been used as a naval base by the German Navy since 1940. The target was the incomplete aircraft carrier, *Graf Zeppelin*, but no hits were recorded. Johnny's operation lasted less than three hours because the aircraft returned with a fuel leak.

> By and large the squadron had just been re-equipped with Lancs and they were looking for a seventh member of the crew, the bomb-aimer, and they were training them locally and so I thought, well I'll have a go at this, particularly since it made a difference of between seven and sixpence and twelve and sixpence a day, so it was worth going for. I had a go and did the course and came back to the squadron as a spare bomb-aimer and flew with crews that hadn't got a bomb-aimer until I joined an all-NCO crew for them to finish off their first tour. And I think it was while I was with that crew that I had one of the few bad experiences in my operational career.

The squadron attacked the Dornier assembly factory at Wismar on both 23 September and 1 October 1942. Johnny was flying with Sergeant Colin Smith and his crew.

> We'd been up to Wismar in the north of Germany. It was the second time we'd been up there and it was exactly the same the second time as it had been the first: absolutely smothered in cloud and so we had these bloody stupid aerial markings, what they called a 'parameter' type of attack. So we'd done this and we were coming back and we'd got just below 10,000 feet, so oxygen masks were off and suddenly there was a blinding flash, completely ruined all night vision, and with the oxygen masks being off they were hanging free and Colin the pilot was fighting like mad to try and control the aircraft that was going down at a hell of a rate of knots. And I remember calling 'Colin, Colin are you alright? Colin, are you alright?' And, of course, Colin daren't take his hand off the controls and so he couldn't get his mask back on to answer. The flight engineer was flashing his light to have a look at the instruments to see what was happening and eventually Colin got it sorted at 2,000 feet – 10,000 to 2,000 in double-quick time, ears hurting like nobody's business. I was sitting in the front turret at

that stage and, as the night vision came back, all I could see were the metal strips. I thought, 'Oh my God, this turret's been burnt out.' But then, as vision really came back, no, it was all there, it was all quite intact. The mid-upper gunner said he could see this St Elmo's Fire creeping along the aerial until it got to just by his turret and then phoof! – off it went. I felt a lightning flash, thank you very much, I didn't want any more of those. I think we were all glad we got back on the ground safely after that. But it was just as well Colin was able to control it, he was good in that respect.

Completing the bomb-aimer's course Johnny had increased his responsibilities during operational flying.

The bomb-aimer's job was twofold. On the route out you manned the front turret. Then you got into the bomb bay as you were approaching the target. You fused and selected the bombs and set your distributor to wherever it needed to be set and you switched on your bomb-sight. People often say to me, were you ever frightened, and I say let me put it this way, I was lying in the front of the aircraft and long before we got there I could see all the gunge that we'd got to go into. I think anybody that wasn't a little bit apprehensive at that stage was either lacking in emotion or else a stranger to the truth. Once we got into the target area my concentration was on the bomb-sight and getting the bombs in the right place. It wasn't easy in the early stages because the Mark Fourteen bomb-sight wasn't the most accurate of instruments, but it was the only one we had. And you were concentrating, it was my job to drop the bombs so I was concentrating on the job I was doing. I was unaware of what was going on round about me and I was directing the pilot to whichever way I wanted him to go. The standard bomb-aimer's jargon was 'left left, steady, right steady' and, as long as it was steady for a while, 'bombs gone'. And we worked together on that so well and we kept it going so that we got as accurate bombing as we could. Once the bombs had gone and we had waited for the camera, as we had to wait for a camera to take a photograph once that was done it was 'let's get the hell out of here' and that was it. And that was basically what the bomb-aimer's job was, to concentrate on dropping the bombs in the right place and then coming back, back up into the front turret, to operate the front guns if necessary.

So when Colin Smith's crew finished their tour I was told I was going to join one Flight Lieutenant McCarthy's crew who was an American.

Joe McCarthy was born in 1919 in Long Island, New York, and famously spent part of his youth as a Coney Island lifeguard. After three unsuccessful attempts to join the US Army Air Corps, McCarthy crossed the border into Canada with his friend, Don Curtin, and joined the Royal Canadian Air Force. He came to England in January 1942 and did his advanced training with 14 OTU. During his 'training' he managed to fly on three operations to the Ruhr on Handley-Page Hampdens. The newly-commissioned Pilot Officer Joe McCarthy joined 97 Squadron in September 1942. His first taste of flying in anger with the squadron was on his 'second dickie' operation to Krefeld on 2 October. He and his crew's first operation together was to Aachen just three days later and when McCarthy's bomb-aimer finished his tour in December there was a vacancy to be filled.

I thought 'Oh my God', because my views of Americans at that stage were not very good. And yet from the first time we met we just seemed to gel. He introduced me to the rest of the crew and we seemed to get on like a house on fire from then onwards. And it went on throughout our time on 97 and into 617. We were getting towards the end of 'forty-two and were still mainly on Ruhr attacks, known as the 'Happy Valley' in those days. It was a question of going into briefing each day and the same target would come up: the Ruhr Valley, Essen, Dusseldorf, Dortmund, wherever, and it was always the same sight, 'Oh Christ not again.' But we went on these and various other trips: Munich, we did a couple of daylights, or semi-daylights, to Italy and then landed in North Africa and bombed Italy on the way back again.

In fact Johnny went on nineteen operations with Joe McCarthy at 97 Squadron through one of the most costly winters that Bomber Command experienced during the war. Their list of operations was one of the most dangerous imaginable, with three trips to Berlin, two to Munich, two to Cologne as well as Essen, Duisburg, Nuremburg and Hamburg. Through it all the crew managed to find a way to work together.

It was primarily the pilot. We had such confidence in Joe as a crew that it welded the crew together. We all gave him the best we could, we did our jobs as best we could, the gunners were good, the flight engineer was good. However, the aircrew depended on their ground crew as much as they depended on each other in the crew. Our ground crew, that was one of the values of the wartime flying, each aircraft had its own ground crew and aircrew and they worked together as a team and our ground crew were always there to see us off and they were always there to see us back. They were a great group and as long as you had that relationship between the ground and the air crews that was more confidence you had. I never felt that I wasn't going to come back and I think that was probably sub-conscious confidence in Joe to start with. But also confidence in the ground crew making sure that [the] aeroplane would get there and get back again and that was all part and parcel of the whole set up of that particular part of the war.

As part of a close-knit crew Johnny was very conscientious about his role as bomb-aimer.

What makes a good bomb-aimer? I think first it has to be confidence in the crew. Knowing that whilst you were doing what you were doing, they were looking after you. Flying, navigating, gunners, whatever. They were looking out for you while you were doing your job. What made a good bomb-aimer was concentration on what he was doing on the bombing run, and he had to concentrate entirely on that at the expense of anything else that might be going on outside. That's what made a good bomb-aimer. I reckon I was one of those.

One heard of people going to a heavily-defended target and getting towards the edge of the defences and then just turning the aircraft and throwing the bombs in. Swinging the aircraft and dropping the bombs at the same time so they were thrown somewhere near the target area. One heard about instances like that. Equipment wasn't very good anyway, so bombing was not in any way really accurate at that stage and an awful lot of bombs fell outside the target area. Basically because people just didn't get there. Sometimes, even if you were concentrating on getting an accurate run, it depended on where you were aiming to start with and how true the bomb-sight was at that time. It depended on putting the correct settings on the bomb-sight before you went into the attack. That's another thing that you had to concentrate on, but there were instances where individuals aborted because they didn't like the look of the target. There were instances of icing being a problem and they had to come back, but there were others where it was just an excuse to come back. Yes, that did happen but I don't think very often. Certainly it never happened with us.

Even the formidable defences of the Ruhr valley could not be allowed to take Johnny's mind off his job.

The defences of the Ruhr were absolutely tremendous and you knew you had to go through hell before you could get back out again. But you still, as the bomb-aimer, had to forget that and concentrate on your bombing run. And the rest of the crew concentrated on their job whilst you were doing that. And it was the one time when the pilot had to do as he was told, of course. He didn't mind that and he responded straight away to whatever instruction I had to give. That was the real reason why it was called 'Happy Valley', of course, and it was the sort of place where I suppose certainly some individuals thought, 'Oh my God, we've had it tonight.' Some did feel like that, I know. And it was actually the same on the Dams raid. I can't remember, certainly not on 97, hearing anybody saying 'Oh God, I'm not going to come back tonight', 'Oh God, no, I can't make it', I never heard that.

The briefing was always the first opportunity the crew got to find out their target for that evening's operation.

You were given an indication of how important the target was at briefing. I don't think, certainly from my point of view anyway, you ever considered what sort of target [it] was you were going to. I don't think, at least I don't think I ever considered what sort of defences it was going to have because I wasn't going to be concerned with them when we got there. It was a question of whether we got hit before we got there as far as I was concerned. But you were given a reasonable brief as to what sort of thing you were going on. The one thing that was often failing in briefings was the Met report, and that was not only true of bomber flying. They had a system where if there was an unexpected wind change then that went out on broadcast to all crews, so the navigators could make whatever changes. Some did, some didn't.

On 2 September 1942 nine crews were detailed to attack the German city of Karlsruhe. Johnny was flying that night with Squadron Leader Coton.

One time I was flying with the flight commander's crew and for the first time we were carrying an 8,000-pounder. Now, several attempts had been made to carry this bomb, not on our squadron particularly but on other squadrons, and either they'd had to come back or the aircraft had been shot down. So there'd never been a successful drop of the 8,000-pounder. So, we were carrying this along, and I was in the mid-upper turret. I happened to look out on the port side and the petrol was pouring out of one of the engines. And so I called up the Skipper and told him and he said, 'Oh God, sorry blokes, we'll have to go back', so the engineer switched the petrol off and feathered the engine and we went back. We landed with the bomb still on, so that was a first.

One of his most memorable raids took place on 28 August 1942. It was a black day for Bomber Command as 159 aircraft attacked Nuremburg and twenty three were lost. On this raid Johnny flew with the squadron commander, Wing Commander J.D.D. 'Joe' Collier. Coincidentally, there were to be a number of connections between the two of them. Before, and for the first year of, the war Collier had flown with Guy Gibson in 83 Squadron. In fact, he flew on two operations when Victoria Crosses were earned: 49 Squadron's Rod Learoyd in August 1940 and 83 Squadron's John Hannah's the following month. Perhaps most coincidental of all was that, when Collier finished his tour of operations with 97 Squadron in early 1943, he worked at the Air Ministry alongside Group Captain Sydney Bufton planning the Dams raid.

And then, the next time we were taking one the Wing Commander decided he would take the Flight Commander's crew. So we went with the Wing Commander. Munich was the target on that particular night and, as we were approaching the target all activity seemed to be going well off to port. And he said, 'Oh those silly sods, they're bombing the decoy.' Incidentally, the navigator on the crew was the squadron navigation officer; he was also the bomb-aimer. There was a time when the navigator dropped the bombs as well. And so we arrived at the target with no opposition whatsoever. So, he went down and he dropped the bomb and then the opposition really came up. And when we got back the Wing Commander was still complaining about people having attacked the wrong target, so the Intelligence Officer, I think he was very wise, said, Well Sir, we shall have to wait till we see the photographs in the morning won't we?' When these photographs came out we hadn't been to Munich, we'd been to Augsburg, only about 40 miles farther south. And this was one of those occasions the nav complained that a wind forecast was sent out and it was a wrong one. The target maps were very similar for Munich and for Augsburg. We took a lot of time to live that one down. Mind you it did show what damage an 8,000-pounder would do because it was the only bomb that was dropped that night.

Given a clear night most aircraft had a good chance of dropping their bomb load on or near the target. However, many times the crews would fly through German defences and marauding night-fighters to find that the targets were obscured by cloud and smoke.

There was bitter disappointment about the weather reports being so badly out and the times that we arrived over a fully-clouded target just wasn't on. I suppose we had to accept that the bomb-sight that we had was the best that we'd got. However inaccurate it may have been you couldn't do anything about it, you could only hope that if you made your settings right then the bomb would go where you wanted it to go. As long as you concentrated on what you were doing then that was the essential.

When Johnny joined the squadron there were still a few Avro Manchesters on the airfield. However, like so many squadrons of Bomber Command in the autumn of 1942, they were re-equipping with Lancasters.

The Lancaster was noisy. It was sometimes smelly. But the bomb-aimer's compartment was probably the most comfortable place in the aircraft. It was such a bloody reliable aeroplane. We never had any doubt about the aeroplane bringing us back provided it didn't get shot up or damaged in action, as it were.

On 17 January 1943 Joe McCarthy and his crew were detailed for an operation to Berlin. They had gone to Berlin the night before and, although it was not a particularly successful raid, the casualty figures were light with only a single aircraft lost. The following night, however, the bomber stream used the same route and this time the fighters and the ground defences were ready.

There was always the danger of fighters. Again we were extremely lucky. We never saw one. And then there was the danger of the defences at the target and some were not so lucky as others. I never did see an aeroplane being blown up over the target. We were only hit once and that was on a Berlin trip and we were hit in the port outer engine and so that was feathered and that was it, and we were flying home on the three without any difficulty. But, then the port inner decided it had had enough and so that too was feathered and Joe needed to fly on the two starboard engines. I know you can trim for some of these things, but you can't trim it all up, you've got to fly the ruddy thing and he flew it back. We were not too far away from the enemy coast when it happened and he flew it back and as we approached the English coast he called 'Mayday'. Tangmere picked us up and it's the only time ever Joe said 'Crash positions', which meant I had to get out of the nose, which I wasn't in the habit of doing. It meant going back to the main spars and sitting down with your back on the main spar. He wasn't sure how the aircraft was going to react when he landed and, for that same reason, instead of landing on the runway he landed to the right of the runway so that, if the aircraft did in fact crumble or whatever, it wasn't going to block the runway for other aircraft. That was typical of Joe's thinking. He thought so much about what he was doing and thought so much about the crew, what he was doing for the safety of the crew. He was a tremendous pilot, he really was. He was big in size, very big in size, six feet six, I think he was; big in personality but also big in ability which was a tremendous boost to the rest of the crew.

The crew's final operation of their first tour was on 22 March 1943 when twelve Lancasters from 97 Squadron joined almost 350 bombers from other squadrons to bomb the docks at St Nazaire on the Atlantic coast of France. It was an uneventful operation and the crew was looking forward to some leave. Johnny had even booked his wedding during his leave. McCarthy was awarded a DFC for his courage and efficiency on the squadron, something that had been noticed by the commanding officer of a brand new squadron that was forming a few miles away at Scampton.

The practice then was the first tour was thirty operations. After which time you went on a week's leave and then you went on to a ground duty until you were called back for operations if necessary at a future time. And since we were coming to the end of our tour my fiancée and I had arranged that we would get married in that week of leave that we had at the end of the tour. So we'd agreed on the third of April as being our wedding day. Joe called us together one day and he said, 'Wing Commander Gibson has had me in and he's asked if I was prepared to join a special squadron that he was forming for just one trip and I said I would have to ask the crew.' And so he was asking us then and we said yes we would go with him for that one trip and so I wrote to Gwyn and said don't worry, it's just one trip, I'll be there. I got a quick message back, 'If you're not there on 3 April, don't bother.' I thought, 'Oh Christ, the first mandate's been issued and that's it.' However, that was fine, no problem, until we got to Scampton and one of the first things we were told was no leave. 'Now I am in trouble.' Anyway, Joe, in typical American style, took us all up to Gibson's office and he said in his inimitable American way, 'We've just finished our first tour; we're entitled to a week's leave. My bomb-aimer's supposed to be getting married on the third of April and he's gonna get married on the third of April.' We got four days so I got there for the third of April and that was it.

During the war the rules for married couples in the Royal Air Force were very strict. However, they didn't stop Johnny and his new wife from organising regular 'brief encounters'!

After we had been married we weren't allowed to live on the same station. Aircrew were not allowed to live with their wives on the same station, so Gwyn was down at Newquay when we were married and she was posted up to Ingham, which was just across the hedge from Scampton, a compassionate posting don't you know. She was a telephone operator and the signals officer came down from Hemswell, which was Ingham's base station, and he said you're too good for here; I want you up at Hemswell. And so she went up to Hemswell and we would meet up if we could in Lincoln. There's eight miles difference between Hemswell and Scampton and the buses both left Lincoln at the same time, one for Scampton, one for Hemswell, and that was always at nine o'clock, that was the last bus, and I invariably ended up at the Hemswell bus and I walked back to Scampton. God, the things one will do in young love in those days.

Joe McCarthy's crew was not the only one to arrive at 617 Squadron from 97. In fact, three crews with distinguished records at 97 Squadron were in the original group that arrived at Scampton in the spring of 1943. Les Munro had completed a successful tour at 97 Squadron at the same time as McCarthy and David Maltby, who was to lose his life on the ill-fated Dortmund-Ems Canal raids in September 1943, and was only just starting his second tour at 97 Squadron when transferred to 617.

It *was* a good squadron. Mind you it was a good Group. Five Group was *the* group in Bomber Command and they proved it with the way they carried out their bombing trips.

No. 617 Squadron would prove to be a squadron like no other these crews had ever flown with. There were plenty of surprises to come.

We just went. And then surprises started. First the shock of no leave was the bad one. The next was seeing so many experienced crews there, many of whom had done their first tour. Some were either doing or had done even their second tour. 'Gongs' all over the place. Why a squadron built up of so many experienced people? That was the first surprise.

The next one was the security. All letters were censored and even the telephone box outside the camp was monitored. We had a squadron evening meeting when Gibson absolutely floored a young Canadian pilot officer for having rung his girlfriend in

Lincoln the night before and said sorry he couldn't make it because we've got something on. That, for Gibson, was a breach of security and he really went to town on him. And to the rest of us we knew exactly what level security had got to be.

I suppose the next surprise was knowing it was going to be low-level flying. That was great. Having been at 10,000, 12,000 or maybe 15,000 feet occasionally and sometimes at a push even higher, the prescribed height was going to be 100 feet. Wha'hey! For me lying in the front that was absolutely exhilarating, just lying there and watching the old ground going Woooof! Woooof! Wooooof! straight past. Whereas I had been sitting on top of those bloody clouds when you could see nothing until you got to the target and then all you saw was rubbish. So that was the next surprise. And as I say the prescribed height was 100 feet, but it was very often much lower than that. Then the aircraft arrived and the first question was 'do those bloody things fly?' Because they'd lost their mid-upper turret, they'd lost their bomb bay as such, and they'd just got these two arms sticking down just behind the nose. 'God, what's that?' And one of them had got a wheel on it. 'What the hell are these things about?' And then the bombs arrived and they were just glorified dustbins and it became obvious that those arms were going to carry those bombs. That was one thing we were able to work out for ourselves. Then there was a question of how we were going to do our exercises? All navigation had to be done by map reading. The bomb-aimer and the navigator would each have their own maps, the nav would suggest what they were supposed to be looking for and I would be looking for it. If I could see it that was it, if I couldn't I would look for something else that I thought was an equal pinpoint and he would be able to adjust according to that. Some crews, when the route was drawn in on the map, cut it down to just either side of that route and put it on a roller so they unrolled it as they went along. But Don McLean and I felt 'sod that', if we should get way off track we would have no idea where we were, so we'll stick to the maps, so we both had maps and that was it. We did our low-level cross-countries and one thing that upset me a little bit about it was that one of the routes went over the Spalding tulip fields and as we went over the poor old tulips went phhhf! I'm sure there must have been a hell of a compensation paid out on that because I can't imagine those growers allowing that to happen without complaining most bitterly.

The other peculiar thing was that we had to make our own bomb-sights. The bomb-sight consisted of a triangle of plywood with a pin in each of the corners. There had to be a specific distance between the two in the base pins. There had to be a specific distance from between the middle of those two to the apex pin. Why, God only knows. And then poles were set up on the target area, which was Wainfleet bombing range. They were set up at a particular distance and the idea was that you put the one pin to your eye and, as you flew, directed the aircraft to bring the two pins in line with these two posts and then you dropped your bomb. We used practice bombs for that. They were plotted by the range staff and when they came back, if they were anything other than very close to the right place, you were in a bit of 'limbo'. You had to explain why it had happened and get out and do some more but quick.

We also did a lot of flying across various dams across the country. Derwent Dam was the main one that was used. I think Uppingham Lake was another one. Derwent Dam had its towers so that was a suitable target sighting arrangement. Uppingham Lake didn't, so they arranged two poles on the dam itself and these were used as sighting exercises. Other dams were used and so that was the day-flying bit. On one of the routes there was a place called Sutton Bridge. Before you got to it coming up from the south the electric cables went over the canal as well. The practice used to be to go under the cables and then up over the bridge. That wasn't scheduled but it was bloody good fun doing it. That was a typical sort of thing, I suppose stupid thing, that we did, but it was great. Nobody got hurt doing it. And having finished most of the daylight training, we then went into simulated night-flying with blue Perspex put around all the front Perspex on the aircraft, bomb-aimer and navigator and pilot's positions. The pilot and the bomb-aimer wore night-vision glasses, which created a sort of dusk effect and so we went on then doing our cross-countries with that simulated night-flying until we then graduated into the actual night flying itself. And, of course, that had to be done in moonlight. It was hopeless trying to do map reading in dark nights so it had to be moonlight when we did that.

617 Squadron, like so many of the Bomber Command squadrons, had many nationalities represented among the aircrew. Despite the possibility of friction inside and between crews there were very few instances of trouble.

In the training for the Dams raid we were coming back from Wainfleet bombing range on one occasion and we were coming back at something like thirty feet. Somebody flew underneath us and Joe wasn't very happy about that because the slipstream could've caused a mid-air collision. We got back and we were convinced that it was Les Munro who had done it. He denied it at first and then he sort of got around to 'well I suppose it might have been possible'. That was it. But after that he and Joe were the best of friends and stayed that way for the rest of their time. You've got American mixing with New Zealand without any problem whatsoever. Yes, I think by and large the mix was good. I don't think there was a lot of national bias amongst any of them or any of us for that matter. You got the odd crack now and again about 'bloody limeys' or whatever, but you gave just as good as you got and it went that way.

In our crew, Joe was an American, Don McLean the navigator was a Canadian, Dave Rodger, the rear gunner, was a Canadian, Bill Radcliffe was a Canadian in the RAF. So, that left three of us Englishmen, Ron Batson, the mid-upper gunner, Len Eaton, the wireless op, and Joe Soap. But we all got on extremely well together and the mixture not only of nationality but of rank had no feeling whatsoever; it had no meaning whatsoever to any of us and that was the way it worked as a crew. Certainly there was no distinction whatsoever. We were all Christian names right throughout the crew, including Joe. And there was no standing off, nothing that suggested there was any difference between any of us. How that went with other crews I don't really know, but certainly with Gibson he wasn't able to bring himself down to talk with the NCOs and certainly not the ground crews. However, that was just his reaction. I don't think there was any real distinction throughout most of the squadron.

It was all very well training for a solid six weeks but still the crews had no idea of their target and no idea as to how their strange new weapon would work.

We discovered on the Saturday night before the actual raid. Barnes Wallis showed us the film of his development of the bouncing bomb and so we learnt that the wheel on the edge was attached by a belt which went back into a bit of the bomb bay to a little JAP engine and that was going to revolve the bomb backwards. It had to be backwards. If it revolved forwards it would have gone straight in when it was released. Rotating backwards, it had to be revolved at 500 revs per minute and it had to be dropped from sixty feet. It started out at a 150 feet, this was when they were doing the trial and it was so obvious that it was going to break up on that and so they came down and Barnes Wallis said to Gibson, 'Do you think your boys would be able to drop from 60 feet?' and Gibson said, 'Ah well, we'll give it a try'. So then there was a question of calculating the exact sixty feet and this is where the lights were introduced. Situated underneath the aircraft, angled so they converged at exactly sixty feet that had been calculated, I think, by the boffins at Farnborough. And so that was the set-up for it.

No crew was happy about going into an attack, low-level, with extra lights, and spotlights at that, blazing out from underneath their aircraft. It was, however, the only way that they could guarantee to be flying at sixty feet at the moment they dropped the bomb.

The operation became very much a team work. The navigator looked through the Perspex at the side of the aircraft looking at the lights, he gave directions up and down until those lights were coincident. The flight engineer was calling out the speed because I think the speed was something like groundspeed 220 knots. So he was calling out the speed and the bomb-aimer was giving directions. The pilot was having to do very much as he was told. Because we'd lost the mid-upper turret the mid-upper gunner was flying in the front turret. Fortunately he'd got a pair of stirrups so he wasn't kicking me in the head all the time.

[The aircraft] just turned up. The one thing that they hadn't thought about, since they'd lost the mid-upper turret they decided to put a gun in the belly of the aircraft. God knows what made them think about that because, having done that, there was no way that a gunner was going to be able to sight from that point of view and he couldn't see where he was firing or anything else so they decided no, that wasn't on, but they left the cradle from which it was going to be pivoted. That was still built within the aircraft frame. That was the one thing that went haywire. I don't think there was much else. Once we'd seen Barnes Wallis's explanation, then I think that answered a lot of problems. It solved the question of where the bomb was going to be, how it was going to be released and what it was expected to do when it was released. That was fine. And having seen that, the conjecture then was that it was going to be the big German battleship probably mostly the *Tirpitz* ... how wrong can you get?

Training was complete and it was time for the squadron to go to war. It was Sunday 16 May 1943 and the crews were about to find out their target.

Three o'clock the next afternoon, Sunday afternoon. Tannoy: 'All 617 Squadron to the operations room.' In we went and then we saw these models of the Dams. They had the Möhne and the Sorpe there, but they hadn't been able to finish the Eder in time and so that was the first we knew.

Joe McCarthy and his crew were detailed to attack the Sorpe Dam. It was one of the three dams feeding the Ruhr valley that were to be primary targets that night. The Möhne Dam, together with the Sorpe, accounted for more than seventy-five per cent of the water supply to the Ruhr valley. The Eder Dam, some sixty miles from the Möhne, held back the largest volume of water of all three primary targets. If all three dams could be breached then it was thought that it would have a catastrophic effect on industry in the Ruhr. As well as the loss of hydro-electric power there would be a loss of drinking water, canals would dry up and there would be a massive effect from flooding in the Ruhr valley. To breach all three huge dams there were just nineteen bouncing bombs.

The Sorpe was of different construction from the Möhne and Eder. While the other two were made from huge blocks of granite, the Sorpe was an earthwork with a watertight concrete core. This caused unique problems. First, there was no wall for the bomb to rest against as it exploded. In fact, the dam's dimensions almost defied attack completely. At the top it was a bare ten metres wide but at the bottom of the earthwork it was a staggering 307 metres. The bomb would just run down the earthwork before exploding. Second, the plan was not so much to blast through the dam wall, rather it was to remove the earth and crack the wall so that a leak would start weakening the dam. Over time it was hoped that this crack would expand and the dam would lose its integrity. Barnes Wallis had calculated that it would need five bombs to breach the dam.

> Originally there were five aircraft briefed for the Sorpe Dam operation. The thing that, I suppose, to some degree disappointed us was that all that bombing training we'd done, we weren't going to use because really the Sorpe had no towers so we had nothing to sight on. Also, it was placed within the hills so that you couldn't make a head-on attack anyway. So, we were briefed that we had to fly down one side of the hills, level out with the port outer engine over the dam itself so that you were just on the water side of the dam, and estimate as nearly as you could to the centre of the dam to drop the bomb. We weren't spinning the bomb at all, it was an inert drop. That was the briefing.

McCarthy's aircraft, AJ-Q, was scheduled to take off at approximately 9.30pm on the evening of 16 May as part of the second wave of five aircraft targeting the Sorpe Dam. Unfortunately, the operation did not get off to the planned start.

> The first thing that happened, having got out to the aircraft, our aircraft, the one we'd used in training was 'Q' Queen – it was 'Queen' then not 'Quebec' [in the phonetic alphabet] – and it decided it didn't want to go that night. It developed a hydraulic leak which couldn't be fixed in time and there was only one reserve aircraft. It had arrived at about three o'clock in the afternoon, that afternoon, had been bombed up, it had been fuelled up, it had done a compass swing with the bomb on. There were no lights; there was no time to fit the lights on it. And so when we couldn't get ours started or to go properly Joe said 'For Christ's sake get out of this and get into the reserve aircraft before some other bugger gets there before we do and we don't get to go.' So we dashed out and as he dashed out he caught his parachute handle on the door of the aircraft so we went across with his parachute billowing out behind him. We got out to the aircraft but there was no compass card in it and so he got into a truck, piled

his parachute into the back of it and went back to the Flights. We had a very good flight sergeant there, 'Chiefy' Powell, and when he saw Joe coming to him he said, 'What's the matter Sir?', and Joe said, 'Well, there's no compass card in it.' So he flew off to the air flights and he got the compass card and brought it back. Then, he went to the parachute section because Joe had said he wasn't going to take a parachute. He went to the parachute section and drew another parachute to replace the one that Joe had lost and he put that in the truck. He said, 'Your parachute, Sir!' That was 'Chiefy' telling him he was going to take a bloody parachute whether he wanted to or not but, yes, we were about thirty minutes late getting off.

Settled in the replacement aircraft, AJ-T, they eventually took off at 10.01pm, thirty-four minutes behind schedule. They were a long way behind the other aircraft from the second wave so McCarthy tried to make up time.

Joe opened up the taps a little bit and we tried to make up as much time as we could. As we were approaching the islands, he said he sensed that the gunners would hear the aircraft, that they'd recognise the noise of the aircraft and so they'd be gunning straight away. He could see these two sand dunes so he went down in between them to avoid the flak. We were toddling along just south of Hamm and this goods train was coming at right angles. Toddling along, and Ron Batson in the front turret said, 'Can I have a go Joe?' I think reluctantly Joe said, 'Oh yes, OK' and so Ron opened up with these little 303s in the front turret. What we didn't know it wasn't just a goods train, it was an armoured goods train and it replied with rather more than 303s. We knew we'd been hit. We felt it. We heard it and we felt it but nothing seemed to happen as far as the aircraft was concerned so we just pressed on.

McCarthy and his crew seem to have had a fairly uneventful trip to the Sorpe after their encounter with the goods train.

We eventually found the Sorpe dam. As we were approaching the mist was beginning to develop and it was a bit difficult to find until we actually did find it. Once we got to the target it was absolutely clear, a brilliant moonlight. Then we saw what we were really supposed to do. What they hadn't told us at briefing was that there was a church steeple on the side of the hill from which we were supposed to attack. So, what did we do? Did we get down low and lift a wing to get over that? Joe said, 'Not likely, we'll use that as a marker and we'll go down from there and get down to sixty if we can.' Well, doing that and getting the aircraft in exactly the right position was more than a little difficult. If I wasn't satisfied I called dummy run and we went round again. If Joe wasn't satisfied he just pulled away and left me to call dummy run and away we went round again. The humourist on our crew was the rear gunner, Dave Rodger, Canadian, and after about the sixth or seventh dummy run a voice from the rear turret said, 'Won't somebody get that bum out of here?' And I thought, 'Aye aye.' I learned how to become the most unpopular member of the crew in quick time. It actually took us ten runs to get it right, but on the tenth one I dropped. I said 'bomb gone', from the rear turret 'Thank Christ', and so up we went to avoid hitting the hills on the other side. We couldn't see, Joe and I couldn't see what the explosion was like but Dave could in the rear turret and these bombs, or mines, were fused to explode at a depth of twenty-five feet, so it was going to roll down, hit the edge of the dam and, at twenty-five feet, it would blow up. The bombs themselves were a total of 9,000-plus pounds, of which 6,500 pounds was explosive. So when that went off at twenty-five feet depth it was going to move a hell of a lot of water. Dave said he reckoned that water went up to a height of about 1,000 feet. He said it wasn't only that because 'when it started coming down again the full lot came into my bloody turret so I thought I was going to get drowned as well as knocked around by you people.' We looked around and we came back and we could see that we'd just crumbled the top of the dam. That was all that had happened. Now Barnes Wallis had told us that he thought it would take at least five bombs to crack that dam because of the structure, it was so different from any others. A concrete centre and then it had this tremendous earthen-ware bank on both sides and then more concrete outside of that. We got ours dropped and Joe was circling at about 1,000 feet and a voice from the rear turret, 'For Christ's sake get down, we're a sitting duck for fighters here,. So down we went.

Johnny released their bomb at about 0.45am on 17 May, having spent almost forty minutes doing aborted and dummy runs over the target. Their bomb was accurate but the effect of the blast was to crumble part of the parapet. Just one other aircraft would find the dam that night. Ken Brown was part of the mobile reserve and attacked the dam almost two and a half hours after Joe McCarthy. It was to prove Barnes Wallis right. More than just two accurately dropped bombs were needed to breach the Sorpe Dam.

We came back over what had been the Möhne Dam by which time it had been breached and it was just like an inland sea. There was water literally everywhere. There wasn't much point in trying to map read in that area. It was still coming out of the dam and so there was some satisfaction in seeing that something had really been achieved. We'd heard radio-wise that the Eder had been breached as well. So, we were 'toddling' along home and for some unknown reason there seemed to be a town coming up ahead of us. It shouldn't have been there and we suddenly found ourselves over the Hamm marshalling yards. Well, the Hamm marshalling yards in May of 1943 was not the healthiest of places to be because it was the main centre for shifting all their armament from the factories out to the various parts of the continent. So down he went because the lower we went the less chance the gunners were able to get their guns down to that sort of level. And again a voice from the rear turret, 'Who needs guns? At this level all they need to do is change the points.' He was so good at creating a humorous situation out of something that might not have appeared to be so and it was tremendous for the rest of the crew. He kept us together. So, Joe said 'right', and then Don Mclean said 'Oh dear' as he realised that the only compass card he'd got was the one where the swing had been done with the bomb on board, the one he'd used for the outward journey and, of course, that wasn't quite right for the way back home. And so Joe said that we were going back the way we came in. We weren't supposed to but that was the way we were going out. When we got back we also found out where we had been hit by the goods train. We were starboard wing low and we were gurgling along and Joe was having some difficulty in controlling it. The flight engineer looked out of the window and said 'We've got a flat tyre, skipper.' That shell had gone through the starboard undercarriage nacelle and burst the starboard tyre. A couple of feet either way it would have been into a petrol tank and that would have been the end of McCarthy's crew. Lady Luck was certainly sitting on board that night.

Of course theirs was only one of five aircraft that were supposed to attack the Sorpe and it was not until they landed back at Scampton at about 3.20am that they started to find out what had happened to the other aircraft.

We began to discover why we'd been the only ones there. Les Munro, going in, had been badly shot up over the islands and it had shattered his communications system, internal and external. So he had to come back. Then there was Geoff Rice who was flying low over the Zuider Zee getting out of the flak range when they heard a tremendous bang. The bomb had hit the water and had been pulled off and rolled back underneath the aircraft. It didn't do the aircraft any good either but he managed to get it home. When they came back Geoff called up to get Control's permission to land but Les couldn't. As Geoff was going into land this aircraft came in underneath him. It was Les going in because it was the only way he could get in, so Geoff had to make another circuit and hope by God he could get it back again. Ottley was shot down and Barlow flew into the cables further over. So that was the other four accounted for and the only reserve that got there was Ken Brown. They had even more difficulty because by that time the mist had filled in so much more and they had, according to them, much more difficulty than we had but they did eventually drop.

The only other reserve that was sent to try to do it was Anderson and he just packed up because it got so late and misty. He landed with the bomb on which he shouldn't have done. He was pushed out the next morning. Gibson pushed him back to his squadron straight away. That wasn't good enough. It wasn't a big enough effort. He hadn't tried hard enough.

The story of Yorkshireman Cyril Anderson is a reminder of the pressures that Gibson and all the crews faced in reaching the highest standards of bravery and professionalism in the most challenging of times. Taking off past midnight as part of the mobile reserve, Anderson was sent to attack the Sorpe Dam as so many of the second wave had failed to reach the target. He didn't reach the dam but turned back when mist was obscuring the valleys, making it difficult to find the target. It was also getting lighter and he decided not to risk his aircraft and crew flying over enemy territory in the early morning light.

Contemporary opinion favours the view that perhaps Gibson was unfair on Anderson. He had been selected for 617 Squadron because of his abilities after just nine operations at 49 Squadron. On returning to 49 Squadron after the Dams raid he and his crew completed a further thirteen operations before being shot down and killed on a raid to Mannheim on 23 September 1943.

The days after the Dams raid were just as difficult for the surviving crews of 617 Squadron. Fifty-six men had been lost, of whom, as they were to find out later, three were prisoners of war. By any calculation it was a huge loss and was bound to affect morale.

During those six weeks we were all concentrating on our own crews so we didn't mix. We brushed by each other in the various sections, bomb-aimers and so on and chatted now and again a little bit, but we never got to know anybody properly. I didn't drink in those days so I didn't go into the bars, so I missed the social life on the squadron as well. But the fact that we had lost eight crews, we started out with nineteen briefed, that was damn nearly fifty per cent. Rather a large loss, one which wouldn't have been entertained as far as the main bombing force was concerned. You couldn't afford to lose fifty per cent of your force. We couldn't afford really to lose fifty per cent of ours but we had to. It was shattering and it really upset Barnes Wallis. Gibson apparently said to him, 'No, you didn't kill them. They went knowing that that was the sort of risk they were taking and that is one of the things about operations of this nature. You go out knowing that there is a chance that you're not going to come back. You take that risk. They did that but they were sound in the way they went out and went about it. It was just unfortunate that they weren't able to come back.' I think that eased Barnes Wallis a little bit.

My own feeling was one of satisfaction of having done the best we could. I think it was also that there had been quite a bit of achievement in the whole of the raid itself and I felt that yes, six weeks of training had really been worth it. I think that was my reaction. I think the public reaction was absolutely outstanding. It

was literally splattered all over and it was on the radio and everything. Really spread all over the place.

After many years of reflection Johnny has had plenty of time to sum up
his own feelings about the raid.

> I had four reasons for saying yes I felt the raid was successful. The
> first one was that it proved to Hitler and the Nazi hierarchy that
> what they thought was indestructible the RAF could get through
> and destroy. The second thing was it did delay, not as long we
> would have liked it to do, but it did delay some of his armament
> production. And the third one was that he had to bring in skilled
> workmen from other war work elsewhere to repair those dams
> and I think the fourth, and possibly the most important, was the
> morale effect it had on the people of this country. I don't know
> how much we appreciated when we were doing the raid how
> important it was and it really probably wasn't until we saw the
> papers the next morning where it was plastered all over the head-
> lines and 'Christ, did we do that?' That was the sort of reaction
> that we got from it. There was certainly reaction to the number
> we'd lost. It was something more than dramatic from that point of
> view and people say to me now, how do you feel about having
> been on the Dams raid? I say I feel honoured and privileged to
> have been allowed to take part in that raid and that's the way
> I look at it still. I'm just sorry that we didn't have more success
> with the raid that we had to make. We had the satisfaction with
> knowing we'd done the best we possibly could and that was what
> we went out to do.

For his own part Johnny had no interest in self publicity.

> My own reaction, initially, was for Christ sake shut up. Gwyn was
> at Hemswell at that stage. She'd been off duty and her colleague
> who relieved her came back into the billet. Gwyn said, 'What are
> you doing here?' 'Oh, we've been shut down. Everybody's been
> shut down but there's something on at Scampton.' And she said
> she heard the aeroplanes taking off and she went to see. Then she
> woke up again as the aeroplanes were coming back and she knew
> we had come back. She had that same confidence that nothing was
> going to happen. But that day, the next day we had time off. We

went to, went back to, the little village in Lincolnshire where I was born, a little village called Hameringham near Horncastle and we went first of all to look at my Mother's grave, then we went to the farmer that my father used to work for, and he invited us in and they gave us tea and we talked about this and that and he said, 'What a wonderful raid that was last night.'. I kicked Gwyn under the table . . . don't say a word. I don't know why. We were coming back from Lincoln on the bus the night after and there were characters in the bus talking about it and I said I wish those bloody people would shut up. She said 'Why?' I said, 'We were on that raid,' and she said, 'Were you now? Why wasn't I told?' I said because it was so absolutely secret. Very well . . .

It was on the radio and everything. Really spread all over the place. And as I say, I think that was one of the big benefits that came out of it, the morale effect on the people of this country in that it was another turning point, something of the war going our way. El Alamein had happened a few months before that and then this came along and a big, big change in what had been a bloody awful war for us so far. I think that was one of the biggest benefits of it all.

On 22 June thirty-three members of the squadron made their way from Scampton to London by train for the investiture and for a party given in their honour at the Hungaria Restaurant in Regent Street by A.V. Roe [the manufacturers of the Lancaster]. The awards included a Victoria Cross for Guy Gibson, Distinguished Service Orders for five of the pilots including Joe McCarthy, fourteen Distinguished Flying Crosses and twelve Distinguished Flying Medals, including Johnny Johnson.

The Queen, it was the Queen because the King was in North Africa and I think, I'm not sure, but I think it was the only investiture that the Queen did. We all went down there and since I was not a partying type, we stayed at a bed and breakfast and of course got a taxi, when he came, to Buckingham Palace. He said 'What?' I said, 'Buckingham Palace.' 'Oh, very well.' So we went in. I couldn't tell you now what the Queen said to me. I haven't the foggiest idea. I was so bloody scared, nervous I suppose it boiled down to. All I can remember saying is 'Thank you, Ma'am' and that was it. Gwyn came as a visitor. She was sitting in amongst some naval types in the gallery, as it were, and they were criticising the filth that was around the place, all the dust all over the monuments you know, having a right time with themselves. Gibson's wife was there and that was perhaps about the last time that they were together, because they were split up very shortly after that. And they had a whale of a time. Mind you, going down we had a special coach, going down by rail and, oh, Brian Goodale, [wireless operator in Dave Shannon's crew] he was debagged on the train, he was running up and down the corridor in his underpants. Now when we got to Grantham we had to change. We got a long wait at Grantham. So the lads were up on the engine and they were pouring the oil all over the place. And then when we came back they'd all spent their money on the booze up the night before, the big party they had with A.V. Roe and what have you. And so we stopped, I think it was again at Grantham, and they'd no money for tea and we were the only ones with any money, so we were buying all the buggers tea and buns. I think the reception generally was one of elation, certainly amongst the public and certainly apart from the drama side of it, the satisfaction on the squadron of having done what we were supposed to do, or almost anyway, I think that was the best way to sum it up.

Not everyone was impressed by 617 Squadron's efforts. Also based at Scampton was 57 Squadron. As part of Bomber Command's Main Force they were out on operations regularly and were unimpressed by 617's single operation.

Fifty-seven was the other squadron and we got on, to start with, reasonably well. But, after the Dams' raid we were sat on our backsides for so long that we were christened 'The One-off Squadron', and that was the way they referred to us. And it wasn't until we left Scampton and moved onto Woodhall Spa, where we had the station to ourselves, that we were then back into the general bombing situation. So that was the difference. Yes, I think we were considered to be a bit nonsensical. Yes, we had been used for one and, although it may have been an important one, 'For God's sake, why aren't you doing more of that sort of thing? We're out every night, or words to that effect, why aren't you?'

The leadership of 617 Squadron for the Dams raid had been entrusted to Wing Commander Guy Gibson. He was just twenty-four when he took command, already a veteran of 170 operations and the holder of two DSOs and two DFCs. Gibson was able to bring together a group of experienced aircrews into a great squadron that carried out an immensely difficult task with great dedication and skill. He wasn't always the most popular man at RAF Scampton but everyone, including Johnny, was able to make a judgement on Gibson as a person and as a commander.

> I have to say that my views on Gibson have to be retrospective because he was the Wing Commander, the squadron commander, I was a sergeant. One thing he didn't have was much of an ability to mix with the lower ranks. He was a little man. Yes, he was arrogant. Yes, he was bombastic. But, he was a strict disciplinarian and I think at that stage he was probably one of the most, if not the most, experienced bomber pilots in Bomber Command, and so he had something to be a bit bombastic about. But, I think, when he came to 617 Squadron, when he formed the squadron, he knew he'd got to get more out of the crews than he had been able to get out of crews elsewhere and so I think he calmed down more. If he wanted something for the squadron he would ring Group, they'd say 'No'. So he'd ring Command and they'd say 'No'. He'd ring the Air Ministry and if they said 'No' he said, 'Right, I'll stay in my office until you change your mind' and he did, and eventually they came back and said alright, it might be possible to do it. And so they did it and that was that. So, from that point of view he got what he wanted for the squadron. But, I think the essence of his leadership came on the raid itself where he made the first attack on the Möhne. He was able to assess the defences that were there and then, as he called each aircraft in he flew alongside them. To me that says 'you're doing this, I'm doing this, and we're doing it together'. That to me was the essence of leadership. He was a good leader, there's no doubt. I have to add to that, I wouldn't classify him as my favourite squadron commander. That has to be Leonard Cheshire, a totally different type of man. He was a great squadron commander.

After the Dams raid in May 1943 there was a period of no operations. The squadron needed to recover after losing so many men. New crews arrived and they needed to be trained in the techniques used by the squadron. Gibson went on leave and then left the squadron and was sent on a lecture tour of the United States. He wrote a book of his experiences to that point called Enemy Coast Ahead. David Maltby took temporary command until Squadron Leader George Holden was confirmed as the new commanding officer on 3 August. And so the crews spent their time on training flights around Britain and over the North Sea. Joe McCarthy and his crew were on one such training flight on 10 June.

It was on one of these when we were on an outward leg over the North Sea, how the hell you could map read over the North Sea I don't know but, this had to be a calculated turning point and then come back. As we were going out I was looking down and I called 'Skipper, there's a dinghy down there'. We circled and yes, it was there and there were two characters in it and they were waving like mad. And so the wireless op wired back to base immediately our position and where this dinghy was. We dropped what supplies we could to them; what of our air-sea-rescue stuff that was available that we could get out to them and then we came back again. About two days later we had a signal from the CO of a Beaufighter squadron thanking us for reporting this dinghy. It was two of his blokes that had had to ditch and the launch came out and took them back to the squadron. So that was something that we achieved, we were quite happy with that.

Operations began again on 15 July 1943 when twelve aircraft from 617 Squadron attacked power stations in Northern Italy. McCarthy's target was at San Polo D'enza, north-west of Bologna.

After the raid we went on leave as I recall. The first trip we did afterwards was another low-level, San Polo D'enza, a transformer station in Italy. It was another of the bomb in Italy go on to Blida and then bomb Italy on the way back. We were using the Mark Three hand-held low-level bomb-sight, which was about as much use as a snowball in hell. But we used it and I think we were dropping at something like 600 feet, maybe a little bit lower. We made our attack, and as we made our attack a bomb exploded and the parts that broke away came down and landed at the junction of my bit on the nose with the rest of the aircraft. It just lodged there. Again, a bit more of 'lady luck'. Another piece went underneath the navigator's feet and stuck into the body of the aircraft. It was one of Les Munro's bombs that had done it. Jimmy Clay was his bomb-aimer and they'd been too low when they dropped. But we got away with that one too. That was why we were late coming back from Blida because they had to fix up that nose bit and by the navigator's feet so that was, that was the first trip after the Dams raid.

August 1943 was taken up with yet more training and a move for the squadron from Scampton to Woodhall Spa. In September Johnny was away on a course and was shocked to hear of the results of two attacks made on the Dortmund Ems Canal.

There was a lot of training. But then we had the Dortmund-Ems and Squadron Leader Holden was acting squadron commander at that stage and this question came up; would the squadron do an attack on the Dortmund-Ems? I was away on a bombing-leader's course at that stage. I was fairly certain that most of the pilots said no. It was absolute slaughter, it wasn't worth it, but Holden insisted that the squadron could do it. They sent out eight aircraft, they lost five of them. He was one of the first to go with some of Gibson's crew. They were shot down before they got to the target. Les Knight was able to get his aircraft up so the majority of his crew could bale out but he didn't, he got killed. Dave Maltby was another. I rang up when I heard about the report of the numbers missing and asked if my crew was amongst them. Joe had been sick, although he was adamant that he wouldn't have gone anyway because he didn't think it was in the least bit worth trying to attempt in those circumstances.

It was so heavily defended and it was so difficult to attack, simple as that. And it was low-level as I understand it, I didn't know too much about it, but I understand it was a fairly low-level attack with standard bombs rather than with anything else. Very little damage was done basically because too few of the aircraft got through anyway, that was really what it whittled down to.

I was away on this course but when I came back I heard primarily what the reaction had been when it was suggested and it had been an almost unanimous 'not bloody likely'. There was obviously concern that we had lost so many and particularly since it had been such an unpopular op to try to do. In the view of most people it should not have been attempted.

After the death of George Holden 617 found itself commanded by Leonard Cheshire, a man who left a huge impression on Johnny Johnson.

Leonard Cheshire was, I think, the finest squadron commander I served with throughout my operational career. He came to the squadron having dropped a rank from being station commander somewhere else. I remember the first squadron meeting that he had. He said, 'If you get into trouble when you're off duty, I will do what I can to help you. If you get into trouble on duty I'll make life a hell of a lot worse for you. So we all knew where we stood from there and that was, I think, the best introduction he could have given us. But, he didn't lay on the heavy-handed stuff at all. He worked with all the air crews. He would visit the ground crews at their work and discuss their work with them and he went through them all that way and he was very highly thought of throughout the squadron. He was a great leader. He developed these techniques for marking, for instance, so that efficiency of the squadron was improved. That was his objective, to get things absolutely right. And he, I would say, succeeded in most of what he tried. I think he was a great man.

In Bedfordshire, near the border with Hertfordshire, lies RAF Tempsford, an airfield with a special place in the history of air operations during the war. It was a base for special duty squadrons, most of which were flown in support of the resistance movement in occupied Europe. Agents were flown in and out by Lysander. Arms and ammunition were dropped by a variety of heavy aircraft including Halifaxes and Whitleys. And in December 1943 four Lancasters from 617 Squadron, including that of McCarthy and his crew, were detached from Woodhall Spa and sent to assist with these special duties flights. Two of the crews never returned.

Later on in the month we went down to Tempsford and I had the feeling that we were the only crew that went down on that occasion and we did a certain amount of training down there with this supply dropping business and then we went out on the one trip and there was no reception committee so we came back and then we came back to the squadron. I didn't know what had happened to our Dams raid aircraft. I fondly imagine they'd go back to A.V. Roe and be remodelled into standard Lancs but apparently no, they just went into storage and ultimately they were scrapped, but these three were kept for dropping supplies to the Resistance in France.

In fact the aircraft that Joe McCarthy had flown on the Dams raid was now being flown by Royal Canadian Air Force pilot Gordon Weeden and his crew, dropping arms to the French Resistance. On his first operation from Tempsford, on 10 December 1943, Weeden was shot down and killed along with his crew. More than sixty-five years later Johnny took part in a TV documentary which visited the site of the crashed Lancaster.

It appears, and this came out subsequently when the aircraft bits were found in this field, it appears from an eyewitness in that area that he saw this aircraft going past on fire. It went down to the bottom, turned at the bottom of the valley and it caught a tree as it turned and it ploughed straight into the field. That was it, and the local people got the bodies out and buried them. The Germans took the majority of the aircraft to melt it down for their own metallic uses and it wasn't until some of these bits were being picked up that I think the French historians started it going. They found these bits and we then got the stories from the eye-witnesses and so on. Then, of course, the television programmes got involved. Apparently somebody in the French Resistance wasn't as good as he should have been and the elite German units knew that this operation was going to take place on that particular evening so they moved their anti-aircraft guns up along the route. They shot two of them down and the other aborted and I suppose it came back and the aircraft was eventually destroyed. The rest certainly were. And that's something that surprises me. Almost makes me feel a bit annoyed that they just didn't keep one for a museum piece because there's none of those original aircraft, those aircraft that were designed for the Dams raid, none of them were kept, and they were scrapped. There we are, it was a bit of history they might have kept. However they didn't. When we went out to France, the nephew of the pilot, also called Gordon after his uncle, came out as well. He had been out previously to where the crew were buried originally but then they were dug up and they were buried in one of the central cemeteries. He brought his uncle's logbook and that had photographs and things and everything that was associated with his uncle and we had quite a time there looking at these pieces trying to decide what they were. Very little we could place apart from this structure which had housed the downward firing gun. That was pulled up intact and then, when we were looking through these bits, I picked up this bit of Perspex and I said that looked to me like a piece of the nose dome. I thought, 'I'm going to have that as part of my old home', and I've still got it here. Yes, there were lots of bits there.

As 1943 drew to a close 617 Squadron's training was changing. The squadron, now under the command of Leonard Cheshire, had its own de Havilland Mosquitoes for the low-level marking of its own targets, the first time Bomber Command had allowed a single squadron to mark and bomb the target.

We had our own marking system. Cheshire did most of our marking and I remember the attack on the French armament factory, where he made three low-level runs over the target to give the French time to get out of the factory before the bombing started. The factory was completely destroyed with the bombing. That again was typical of Cheshire.

Gone was the ultra-low-level flying for the Lancaster crews. Instead the squadron received a new bomb-sight and training to bomb with pinpoint accuracy from high level.

High-level training, back to high-level training with the SABS and that was the main part of it. I don't honestly remember doing anything other than doing a lot of higher level training. On 617 we were equipped with the Stabilised Automatic Bomb-sight which was a vast improvement. It was just a question of putting a couple of settings into the bomb-sight, ground speed was one and I think height was the other. But these you set, two pointers, and, as you switched the bomb-sight on, these points went round and when they came together it automatically released the bombs. Provided you fused them and selected them and set the distributor up it was much more accurate because, however much you moved the aircraft, it was gyro-stabilised, it stayed in a steady plane the whole time. That was why 617 became the special target squadron after the Dams raid, because they'd got this superior bomb-sight. And it worked. It was such a tremendous difference. It made a tremendous difference to the accuracy of the bombing.

The first chance 617 had to prove the SABS's effectiveness was against Hitler's new terror weapons, the V-1 'flying bomb' and the V-2 rocket. On 30 December ten aircraft attacked a V-1 'flying bomb' site. Pathfinders dropped markers that landed 250 yards from the target. But, because 617 Squadron's average error on bombing was less than 100 yards, the squadron's subsequent bombing was so accurate that none of the bombs hit the target at all.

The V-1 and V-2 sites came in December because we went after we'd been down to Tempsford. When we came the squadron had been re-equipped with the 12,000-pound HC and the aircraft had been modified to carry it. The first raid that we went on was to the V-2 sites in Northern France with SABS. We had no idea what effect dropping that bomb would have on the aircraft. So we ran in and got to the 'bombs gone' situation, we got a bump, not a big one but we got a bump, and I looked out and plotted a bomb going down and then we came home. One of the bombing checks after a bombing raid was to open a little hatch in the step as you get down into the nose and shine the Aldis lamp in it to make sure that all the bombs had gone. 'Well,' I thought, 'that's bloody silly with a bloody great bomb like that and we had felt the bomb', so I said, 'I suppose I better do it' and I opened up. The bomb was still intact, still carrying it and I said to Joe, 'We've still got a bomb, Skipper'. 'Jesus!', and Don McClean said, 'Let's jettison it,' and Joe said, 'No,' he said, 'either the bomb-aimer's shit or the instrument man's shit and I'm going to find out which it is.' I thought, 'Oh, Christ, I'm in trouble now alright.' And so we got back and reported at de-briefing that this was what had happened. We were going on leave the next morning. I'd just been commissioned and I was going to buy a uniform on that leave. So, we went out to the aircraft before we went on leave in the morning and the bomb was nestling nicely on the bomb cradle underneath. I went inside and the instrument officer was inside and he said, 'Why didn't you jettison it?' I said, 'You must be joking, a single bomb like of that size and you've got to jettison it, don't be bloody silly.' I said, 'What was wrong anyway?', and he said, 'Well your bomb-sight was changed in the afternoon and the instrument man that put it in, instead of plugging it into the automatic socket he plugged it into the manual socket.' I had no idea at that stage that there were two sockets. But I learnt something then and I made bloody sure from then onwards that I looked where the bomb-sight was plugged in, that it was in the right place. But I thought 'thank Christ for that', because I couldn't think what I had done that shouldn't have released the bombs. They'd been selected, everything had been set up, the bomb-sight had been set up, I just couldn't understand why. And I suppose, in retrospect, we should have known the effect of dropping that bomb was going to be more pronounced than the bump that we got and that must have come from the explosion of somebody else's bomb going off. Series of coincidences. But it happened. We went on our leave and I got my uniform so that was fine.

Johnny Johnson continued on operations with his crew right through until April 1944. The winter and spring of that year were mainly taken up with perfecting high-level bombing techniques with SABS and operations against targets in occupied France. Time after time factories producing explosives, aero engines and aircraft were destroyed by just a few aircraft bombing accurately. Johnny had flown on twenty operations with the squadron but now there was a reason to reconsider his future.

Well I think this again illustrates Joe's consideration for crew. Gwyn was expecting our first child. And he pulled me aside one day and he said, 'Johnny, you've got to give Gwyn a chance; she doesn't know whether this child's going to have a father or whether she's going to have a husband, she must be worried stiff. You've got to give her a chance, pack it up now', which meant as far as I was concerned he'd made me realise that I'd got other responsibilities, apart from fighting this bloody silly war that we were in. I hadn't had that responsibility, I hadn't thought about that responsibility too deeply before. But he brought it home. He knew Gwyn and this, I'm sure, was one of the reasons why he said what he said. I don't think it was because he wanted to get rid of me as a bomb-aimer because we got on so well together. But that was typical of Joe. He thought not about me so much but for Gwyn and what I was causing her. And actually, in actual fact she wasn't particularly worried but it was always a chance. And, in fact, when the child was born she had a seventy-two-hour labour period. He was a big bugger, ten-and-a-half pounds.

So that was why I left the squadron at that stage. I didn't want to leave the crew but I had to accept that, yes, I had got other responsibilities and that was why I started the various instructional professions that I went through. Doing the instruction rather than being instructed.

In particular Johnny would miss flying and working with Joe McCarthy.

Joe had a tremendous respect for the rest of the crew and consideration for the rest of the crew. When he died the only reason I knew was I read his obituary in the *Telegraph* so I wrote to Alice, his wife, or his widow rather, and expressed my condolences. And when she wrote back she said you may not know it but you were his favourite. And that to me meant what I thought in the first place: we seemed to gel from the moment that we met.

Johnny was finally posted away from 617 Squadron on 6 May 1944. For the rest of the war he instructed at various RAF bases: No. 1 Air Armament School at RAF Manby and then onto 1654 Heavy Conversion Unit at RAF Wigsley just a few miles from Scampton and Woodhall Spa. Throughout his time with the RAF during the war he was a huge fan of the Lancaster bomber and enjoyed instructing other crewmen to get the best out of the aircraft.

Without a doubt the Lancaster was the finest bombing aircraft in the war, including the American stuff. We had a lovely song which talked about 'Flying Fortresses at 40,000 feet. But we've only got a teeny weeny bomb, glory, glory what a hell of a height to fly'. So the answer then 'flying Avro Lancasters at zero-zero feet, and we've got such a bloody great bomb', and that was repeated several times. That was the chorus of that relationship between ourselves and the Army Air Corps, basically because that was not a good relationship. They did twenty-five trips for a tour and they went off home again. We had to do thirty. They did daylight raids rather than night raids and for that they had quite a lot of fighter escort when they went out. They seemed to be better protected than we were. However, that again was part and parcel of the war. When the Army Air Corps came over here they asked Joe to transfer. Now Joe was a very good drinker and he got himself well and truly 'thank you very much' before he went down for his interview and he told them what the bloody hell they could do with their Army Air Corps. So he didn't get transferred, but he didn't want to go.

Johnny finds it quite easy to sum up his whole wartime experience, and in particular his time at 617 Squadron.

It was a period of, I think, complete satisfaction, of having such a good crew to work with and such a capable and conscientious pilot and the satisfaction of having done the job that we were supposed to do. I have felt I had done my job properly as had the rest of the crew. And there was that satisfaction about it.

The real crux of the whole of my operational career was the Dams raid. Had I not had that, that would have been missing and it would have been something which, for me, was the highlight of my operational career. What would it have been like without it? I don't know. It would probably have been a question of accepting what I was supposed to do and getting on with it. But not having the satisfaction of having had that sort of operation to go through – it would have been better when we got onto the post Dams raid work – but had it just stayed at Main Force stuff, I don't think it would have been very thrilling at all.

Johnny Johnson stayed in the Royal Air Force until September 1962 when he retired with the rank of squadron leader. In the years after the war he had spent time with 100 Squadron on Lancasters and Lincolns before moving into maritime aviation with 120 Squadron when they were converting from Lancasters to Shackletons. His final posting was at RAF Hemswell where, coincidentally, the squadron in residence was 97, now radically changed from its wartime bombing role to a Thor IRBM missile unit.

Johnny is very positive about the roles played by both the Lancaster and 617 Squadron during the war.

I think the legacy was that a squadron had been able to achieve what they did achieve so much against the odds and I think that's the legacy that they left along with the thwarting of the German attempts. The Lancaster's legacy, however, comes from the people that flew in them and their satisfaction with the aircraft they were flying in because it was, again, personal. It was the best, no doubt about that, that's its legacy. It was the best, not only British, it was the best bomber aircraft that we had.

George 'Johnny' Johnson still enjoys talking about his wartime exploits and has spent many hours with enthusiasts of all ages. At the time of writing, he is the last survivor of the Dams raid living in Britain.

Pilot Officer George "Johnny" Johnson – Operations at 617 Squadron

- 16/17 May 1943 – Sorpe Dam – Johnson dropped his bomb accurately but, although the top of the dam crumbled, it was not breached.
- 15 July 1943 – San Polo D'enza Electrical Transformer Station. Target partially obscured by mist and was not destroyed. The twelve Lancasters of 617 Squadron bombed and then flew on to North Africa, landing safely at Blida.
- 24 July 1943 – Leghorn [Livorno] – Dock and harbour installations. Bombing was carried out on the return journey from North Africa. Again mist obscured the target and bombs were dropped on the estimated position of the marshalling yards.
- 29 July 1943 – Milan – NICKEL raid dropping leaflets on Italian cities. Again the aircraft were flown on to Blida and returned between 1 and 8 August.
- 20 December 1943 – Special Operation – Supply drop to French Resistance from Tempsford. Target could not be found so mission abandoned.
- 22 December 1943 – Special target – Flying-bomb site. Mission abandoned.
- 30 December 1943 – Special target – Flixecourt flying-bomb site. Accurate bombing but dropped on misdirected markers. Target not destroyed.
- 21 January 1944 Special Target – Flying-bomb site. Target attacked successfully.

- 25 January 1944 – Special Target – Flying-bomb site. Target attacked successfully.
- 2 March 1944 – Albert – Aircraft factory. Very successful operation with the factory virtually destroyed.
- 4 March 1944 – St Étienne – la Ricamerie needle-bearing factory. Operation abandoned as target was not located due to cloud.
- 10 March 1944 – St Étienne – la Ricamerie needle-bearing factory. Operation only partially successful as target only slightly damaged. Many of the markers bounced off the factory.
- 15 March 1944 – Woippy – Aero-engine factory. Operation abandoned as target obscured by cloud.
- 16 March 1944 – Clermont-Ferrand – Michelin tyre factory. Very successful precision raid. Leonard Cheshire flew over the factory three times to warn French workers. Target destroyed.
- 18 March 1944 – Bergerac – Explosives factory. Factory completely destroyed.
- 20 March 1944 – Angouleme – Explosives factory. Target completely destroyed.
- 23 March 1944 – Lyons – Aero-engine factory. Results could not be assessed.
- 25 March 1944 – Lyons – Aero-engine factory. Not a complete success with scattered bombing.
- 5 April 1944 – Toulouse – Bréguet/Latécoère aircraft factories. Squadron acted as markers for the Main Force. The first low-level Mosquito marking flight of the war. Target destroyed.
- 10 April 1944 – St Cyr – Signals depot. Very successful operation. Target destroyed.

George 'Johnny' Johnson was posted from the squadron on 6 May 1944.

Chapter 4

Pilot Officer John Bell

As a small boy John Bell enjoyed watching aeroplanes coming into a local field near his home in Essex. Following a move to Surrey, John left school aged sixteen just as war was declared in September 1939. Like many at the time, neither John nor his family thought that the war would last long and so it was decided he would start work with a firm of chartered accountants in the City of London.

Not wanting to feel left out of the war effort John joined the local Home Guard in which he was trained how to carry out acts of sabotage to be used in the event of a successful German invasion.

For two years before I joined the Air Force I was a member of the Home Guard, so I was doing a bit of parading around with a rifle and no bullets and in the appropriate uniform. But I didn't care for it very much. So I thought the blue attracted me far more.

Part of the training was carried out over a number of days at Roehampton, where we were taught all sorts of things like putting sand into the hot-boxes of railway engines. If the Germans were going to invade we were going to be helping behind the lines. I didn't understand how this was going to happen. I also enjoyed going to Bisley and shooting there so that I could use the rifle. So yes, there was a certain amount of apprehension in those days, wondering what was going to happen during 1940 when the thought of an invasion was quite pre-eminent in people's minds.

During the Battle of Britain I did travel around Kent several times with another accountant and there was always an aerial dogfight going on during the day during the middle of the year. Well for a young person like me, watching it all, we weren't actively involved and we weren't in danger of any attack from bombs falling on us, so it was quite exciting.

Spurred on by seeing the live air combat in Kent skies and tales that his friends told of their experiences John made up his mind he would join the Royal Air Force.

Two or three of my friends, older friends joined the Air Force and they came back with tales of flying Whitleys and things, and I was very air minded anyway, so I decided that I wasn't going to join the Army, I didn't fancy tramping through fields of mud, so I joined the Air Force. I was keen to be a pilot, obviously, but I was deemed to be too long in the leg and not able to get out of a cockpit in a hurry so I had to train as a navigator which in fact turned out to be an observer. And so that's how I got into the Air Force.

I think my family were a little bit, I'd say, perturbed about what was going to happen as, naturally, people were being called up. By 1941, when I was able to volunteer, some battles had been going on and it was obviously of concern to them but they knew I'd have to go eventually since I was eighteen and, rather than wait to be called up, decided to volunteer so I think they accepted it in that respect.

With the decision now made and accepted by his family John had to wait until he reached the minimum qualifying age of eighteen and a half. He finally joined up in June 1941.

I went to a recruiting office in Worcester Park, Surrey and joined up and came back and told my family I'd done this. I think there was a great amount of surprise. Then I had to wait for an interview. I went to Oxford for a medical and for the interview and that's where, having measured me in various parts of the leg, they decided that navigator was going to be my career if I still wanted to join the Air Force or still wanted to volunteer as this was a voluntary act for air crew.

Call up came in September. That was three months after I had my medical and volunteered. So I started with four weeks, the usual thing, at Air Crew Reception Centre at Lords and then a period of three or four months in Torquay on 13 ITW [Initial Training Wing]. From there I moved to Eastbourne to a course mainly concerned with navigation. And then some months later, I think in May, I sailed with a number of other people to South

Africa and eventually finished up at 45 Air School, Oudtshoorn, where I trained as an observer. This course covered not only navigation but bombing. Gunnery was conducted separately at Fort Alfred.

Being in South Africa was only part of the training scheme as aircrew were being trained in Canada and South Africa. I was quite pleased to be going there because I knew nothing about South Africa and had never been overseas before going there and whatever I thought about Africa was completely wrong. I enjoyed the time there. I liked the weather and flying was easily controlled because of the good weather we had down there. And I really thoroughly enjoyed it.

At gunnery school the flying was conducted in Airspeed Oxfords with a turret at the back where you could stand up and there was something called a Scarff ring which stopped you shooting the tail off the aircraft because you had to elevate the machine gun which happened to be a Lewis. That meant we were shooting at drogues towed behind other aircraft. You had to manipulate the gun and tilt it up to move it across the over the Scarff ring and down the other side. I thought I'd be clever and lift it out ánd put it down myself whereupon of course my hand stuck to the barrel. I didn't do my hand very much good picking up a red-hot barrel.

John returned from South Africa on a liner being used as an American troopship which came to England via New York and then across the Atlantic.

Eventually I turned out as an observer, came back to England early in 1942, found myself at Cottesmore, 14 OTU, ready to join up with a crew. When I came back to England I was informed that I was going to be bomb-aimer, having trained as an observer. I don't think that bothered me too much because I am rather a hands-on person, and it seemed to me that was a better career move.

The standard bomb-sight for RAF Bomber Command since the start of the war had been the Mark IX. It was an upgraded version of a First World War design which worked fine but only if the aircraft could fly straight and level to the target on a pre-arranged course. Manoeuvring to miss flak and fighters or changing course meant that bombing accuracy was considerably below the required levels.1942 saw the introduction of the new Mark XIV, which was much easier to set and quicker to reset if the aircraft had been forced to manoeuvre on the run to the target.

When we came back and joined OTU [Operational Training Unit] the first part of the course was bombing. That was carried out separately at another airfield and the navigation aspect of the course took place after that. And the bombing course was when I first came face to face with a Mark XIV bomb-sight, having been trained on the Mark IX in South Africa. It was only recently that I looked at my logbook to check the comparative results of bombing and I found that I was much more accurate with a Mark IX bomb-sight, getting an average area of around some fifty yards, whereas with the Mark XIV at OTU, I was getting somewhere around 160 yards. Perhaps this was something to do with not being completely familiar with the way they operated it. But, it seemed to please the directing staff in as much as they gave us quite a high course result assessment and an extra week's leave, because we completed the course in good time and to their satisfaction. So perhaps that's the way that they felt that crews under training would achieve that sort of level and it would be adequate for Bomber Command.

From there we went to heavy conversion unit and first of all we converted onto the Manchester. Now, of course, this was a delightful aircraft, I thought, after flying in Wellingtons. There was a lot of room and it flew nicely. Clearly it had problems with the engines, although we didn't experience any and, within a few weeks of heavy conversion, the Lancaster came into the course and we then transferred. So by the time we met up on the squadron in June '43, we felt pretty confident, although apprehensive of what lay ahead of us.

The first time we got into a Lancaster was at the heavy conversion unit. After flying in the Wellington, which was alright but they weren't in very good condition at OTU, we were pleased to get a bigger aeroplane. I liked the Lancaster, I liked everything about it except the long trek back to where the Elsan [chemical toilet] was at the back of the aircraft. From my point of view, I suppose I had more room than the rest of the crew. I could stand up and lie down and had room on either side. I thought it was a good aircraft and the more I flew in it the happier I was with it, very robust, never gave us any trouble, never really had any trouble with the engines. It was manoeuvrable. As a bombing platform I thought it was very good.

One of the regular procedures at OTU was crewing up.

Crewing up was a standard procedure, I believe. At OTU we just assembled in a hangar and there were pilots and rear gunners and bomb-aimers and navigators all milling around and we were told to form up in a crew. So you stood around looking rather bemused, wondering who you're going to fly with. I was standing talking to a Canadian navigator wondering who we would get as a pilot when a chap came up to us looking as bewildered as we were. I remember we were only twenty-one or so and he said, 'Have you got a pilot?' I said, 'No, we haven't got a pilot yet, we're looking around.' He said, 'Well I've found a chap and I've done a bit of investigation', [he was the rear gunner] and he said 'I've found this chap. He's had a crash during his training in an Oxford and he looks as though he might look after us fairly well, he's probably learnt from that experience, so I'll take you over.' So he took us over to Bob Knights, as we found out, and said, 'I've found you a navigator and a bomb-aimer'. 'Oh good,' said Bob, 'so all we need now is a wireless operator.' Off he went and he found a wireless operator and that's how we crewed up. Now the rear gunner was named Peter Derham and he was twenty-nine years old, so he was much senior to us, much older, and we treated him as an older person. We called him 'dad' in fact. And we always look back on that episode where he went out and found a crew for the pilot and, having found the pilot for us, he then found a crew. And I suppose that was written in the stars somewhere, that we had the right pilot.

Bob Knights was born in London in 1921. He volunteered for the RAF and was called up in early 1941. Trained as a pilot under the Arnold Scheme in the United States he had been forced to bale out of his aircraft twice, once in Florida and once after returning to the UK.

Bob Knights was a very nice person. He'd had a lot of experience with flying. He'd done his training out in America and was a very competent pilot. He was not a strict disciplinarian but he let us know what he wanted us to do and he could be upset if we weren't there at the time he wanted us to be. But we got on extremely well; he was a very good friend. We acknowledged very quickly that we had a good pilot with us. He quickly learned the tricks of his trade that on operations you do certain things, you don't just fly straight and level all the way to the target, you move around, and I think he was taught this by the pilot he flew with on his initial 'second-dickie' trip once we joined the squadron [pilots went as second pilot with another crew before their first operation with their own crew]. He never let us forget that we should be observing whatever went on around us and to report back to him if we saw anything untoward; in other words, to keep up a flow of information. After the war, and it was some time after the war, I met with him again and then with the Squadron Association. We met up fairly frequently, he and my family. We always had that rapport, friendliness and rapport between each other.

The rear gunner was a very alert man. He took his job very seriously. Remember it was very cold at the back end of a Lancaster but he plastered himself up, all the exposed parts of his face and hands, with lanolin. I remember him having this lanolin spread all over himself and he just always kept up a running commentary of what was going on around him, what he could see, or thought he could see and so we felt pretty safe having him there.

I never had any regrets at all with that crew. It was a good crew. Most crews gelled eventually; you had to learn to trust each other. We all came from different backgrounds. We just went as a family everywhere. Naturally two or three of you would join up and go out drinking or out to a party or whatever, but generally the whole crew went out and it was that sort of crew, you just stayed together. I never had any qualms about any of them. I hope they didn't have any qualms about me. But we all seemed to fit in. I think the force of circumstances meant that you had to; you had to get on with people considering the job you were doing.

Being together, both on the ground and in the air, was more than just a case of 'getting on'. As the crew socialised together, close-knit relationships and a bond of trust developed that was critical to their performance as an operational air crew, in particular where it counted – in the air on operational sorties.

The crew working together, first of all, have to have confidence in each other's job. Particularly the gunners who are looking out everywhere around the aircraft to keep the pilot informed of any fighter activity when we're on operations. The navigator, we really had great confidence that the navigator was making sure he knew where he was. Our Canadian navigator was very good. His name was Harry Rhude. His father was also in the Canadian Air Force and came over during the time we were together. His father was a wing commander and he kept tabs on his son. Unfortunately, I lost track of him after the war when he went back to Canada.

But it was having that respect of the rest of the crew. You know who they are and you just mix with them and there wasn't any one member of the crew that I wasn't afraid to talk to or be with.

After all his very thorough and detailed training John and his crew were ready for their first operational posting. No. 619 Squadron had been formed in April 1943 and was based at Woodhall Spa in Lincolnshire.

When we left the heavy conversion unit we knew we were posting to 619 Squadron, we also knew it was a fairly new squadron. It had been formed about two or three months before we joined it. So, it was a question of excitement, you'd done all your training and [were] now heading for the operational end of the flying training, wondering what the squadron was going to be like. I remember our first thoughts when we arrived at Woodhall station and were waiting for transport. Bob had gone to telephone to say we were there and wanted transport and I remember him saying, 'I wonder how long we're going to last here?' which wasn't a very good thing to perhaps think about but, nevertheless, our thoughts were that it was not going to be an easy run.

Joining the squadron, I seem to remember, was fairly easy. We were put into a particular flight, probably A Flight. However, it was Bob's responsibility, of course, to organise us. We were then put under the control of the bombing leader and a navigational leader and a gunnery leader and wireless operator, so we each were separately further instructed by our particular overseers. There was a fair amount of flying to be done, flying training, and particularly bombing training at Wainfleet; further familiarisation with the bomb-sight. Then Bob did the first of his two 'second dickie' trips with the experienced crew. After that we just settled into what seemed like a routine.

Life on the station, as I recall, was very easygoing. There were no parades, or I can probably remember about one parade when we were stood down for a period and there were other activities going on like cricket games and football and so on. Apart from being at certain places at a certain time for briefing or for training or for servicing the aeroplane, it was a pretty free sort of existence. It was unusual, having gone through initial training in the air force where you had to be in a certain place at a certain time and you were marching and you were on parade and drilling and so forth; it was quite different. And so you got this sort of relaxed atmosphere and the atmosphere only heightened during the days when you knew you were on an operation. It was a pretty easygoing sort of life when you weren't on operations. A lot of the time was your own and you filled it in the best way that you could, bearing in mind that you knew that you had to be familiar with a lot of things that were going to be important to you. If you went out as a crew you went out to the pub [and] you'd probably join up with other people but essentially the people you were with were your crew.

John remembers well how the pace changed on the days when operations were on.

They all started out in much the say way in that we knew an operation was going to be planned for that evening or at night. So, preparations during the day were to get the aircraft ready, fly and service it, leave it to be bombed up and fuelled and attend briefings. The briefings all went on in the same pattern: where the route across Germany was determined and if there were any alterations necessary by crews saying in their experience it wasn't a good idea to go that particular way and to change the route slightly to avoid heavily defended areas.

When we knew during the day that a raid had been planned for the night then each member of the crew went off to his particular department. I went to bombing, to find out what the bomb load was going to be and how it was to be dropped, the number of aircraft likely to be in the raid and time of bombing, time we had to be there. So, armed with all that information I would check with the armourers. I didn't oversee the bombing up of the aircraft, but when you're round the aircraft getting it serviced for the raid and we're all involved in our various bits of activity, then you naturally observe the bombing train coming along with all the bombs on board. Before the bombing up of the aircraft took place we had to service the aircraft and make sure it was completely serviceable and take it up for an air test that lasted fifteen or twenty minutes, sometimes half an hour, when you tested all the equipment. I can't remember doing any separate bombing. Practice bombing was done at Wainfleet on a day when there was no operation. So, I was just making sure that things were working at the front end. I also had the turret to manipulate if need be. It was a good place to stand up and stretch one's legs. I think we did a little bit of practice air firing just to make sure the guns were working OK, as did the gunners. So, every man was checking his own bit and my responsibility was making sure that everything in the front end, particularly the bomb-sight, was working correctly.

John's first operation happened to coincide with the first major raid on Hamburg, Germany's second largest city, on 24 July 1943. A total of 791 aircraft took part in the first phase of Operation GOMORRAH, the bombing plan to destroy Hamburg in a series of raids at the end of July.

The first operation we had was on the first raid on Hamburg. It was all excitement with the use of 'Window', the strips of foil that we dropped. That was the first time it was used. I think we just learnt as we went along. I mean you can't do anything else but learn as you're flying, this is the way to go. We gave a lot of thought to it individually and collectively too, what we were doing.

The first raid on Hamburg, our first operation, was quite alarming really. As far as I remember the flight was without incident. We were certainly not the first over the target. By the time we got there it was all ablaze and our markers were going down and aircraft were flying by. If I said it was exciting, it was not what we expected, well at least I didn't. You see, I was at the front of the aircraft getting a full view of everything, so I was quite involved with the bombing run. But at the same time, it was quite an experience to see the city ablaze and our heavy bombs going off and exploding everywhere. It was a tremendous view. I can't forget it. We repeated that two or three times during the week. You wondered how long can this continue?

The first Hamburg operation is indelibly fixed in John's mind.

Before arriving at the target, you were flying over a dark North Sea, dark Germany, above cloud hopefully. The first thing you saw in the distance was the searchlights around the city, exploding shells, ack-ack shells. Then, fires on the ground from the bombing force ahead of you and this was pretty much the same for all the operations. I think also there was a great deal of thought, a lot of apprehension. My abiding thought approaching any target on any of the operations with the Main Force was seeing the fires of the city and the sky filled with shell bursts. The smoke they left behind would be illuminated by the searchlights. You had a wall of fire in front of you which you had to pass through. I wasn't afraid but I was apprehensive about it. I just thought 'how are we going to get through that?' It happened time and time again. Then you just concentrated on the bombing run and ignored everything around you and when you came out the other side, breathed a sigh of relief and told the pilot to climb a bit higher and get out.

At the end of a week of concentrated bombing against Hamburg the city was almost completely destroyed. The weather was hot and dry and the mainly wooden houses went up in flames causing a firestorm that engulfed vast areas. Over 40,000 people were killed and another million made homeless. Great numbers of people fled the city and industrial production never reached pre-raid levels during the rest of the war.

The targets at 619 Squadron, as part of Bomber Command's Main Force, varied. Hamburg sticks in my mind because those were the first ones we attacked. Berlin I remember vividly, the number of times we went there. Others were targets in the Ruhr that I can't individually remember but they all seemed much the same at the time. The only one that was very bad was Nuremburg where a lot were lost and we had great difficulty with icing up engines. So, the operations over Germany were much of a muchness. They were all pretty similar. Weather conditions varied, of course. So, navigation was either difficult or easier according to where we were going and how far. Of course, totally different from our operations later with 617 Squadron.

The defences were pretty well the same everywhere, very heavy, great concentrations of searchlights, night-fighters, of whom we saw very few fortunately; none attacked us. We were also very fortunate in having only relatively few flak holes in the aircraft – and nothing very serious – except for one time very early. We lost an engine on an approach to Hamburg but that was overheating, it was nothing to do with enemy action.

John Bell's job as bomb-aimer kept him busy for most of the long flights to the targets.

One of the things that was laid down, because of accidents that [had] happened, was that the bomb-aimer on take-off didn't sit down in his position as he was pretty vulnerable and the first one to hit the ground if the aircraft crashed. So I was just standing up behind the flight engineer. But, as soon as we were airborne, I took my place down in the front. Depending on the time of day – whether it was daylight or it was night when we took off – I had some map reading or observing to do to supplement what the navigator was able to do, to help him to keep on track. If there were any identifying features I would try to identify them, otherwise it was a matter of keeping a sharp look out for anything that was untoward, like any aircraft that shouldn't be there.

Coming up to the target was when the bomb-aimer tended to take over with directing the pilot on the run. You had identifying features to aim at, either a pinpoint you could see or markers that you knew you had to aim at. So it was a matter of directing the pilot the last few miles, that we were on the right course, and attend to the bomb-sight. That had to be switched on beforehand so the gyroscope could line itself up and control the bomb-sight. The bomb selector had to be operated to select the bombs and fuse them. I made sure that the information fed into the computer and given to me by the navigator was as accurate as it could be regarding wind direction, drift and so forth, and all the other information that needed to go in to satisfy the bomb-sight. Then, that was it. Taking the aircraft up to the point of release, the bomb doors would be opened – not too early because there was shuddering with the bomb doors open, so they were opened really late. Then, when the bomb-aimer released the bombs, he made sure that all the bombs had gone by looking through the clear panel into the bomb bay. You had to hold it steady for a short while for the photo flash to illuminate and record the photograph automatically. You hoped that you got an aiming-point photograph and then got out of the target area. And that was the end of my job except, of course, to keep a look out on the way back.

Practice was the thing. Familiarity with the equipment, making sure you had the right information put into the computer and that the navigator and pilot knew as much as you did about the information you needed to put in and how accurate it needed to be. Then, confidence in your ability and also perseverance in approaching the target to the point that you knew you had to release the bombs. I suppose it would have been too easy, if you were a panicky sort, to bomb a bit early and some crews did but that was called 'creep back'. It happened when crews would bomb the first bit of conflagration they saw rather than the middle of the target area where they should be aiming at. So I tried to do what we were trained to do and that was to bomb as accurately as possible on and where the aiming point was indicated.

The effect of the bombing was difficult to determine for us because we were bombing from 20,000 feet. We really couldn't see the effect of a particular bomb blast except that you could tell that a 4,000-pound 'cookie' had exploded because of the amount of explosive, the detonation you could see from that height. Dropping practice bombs was quite different; they were just 11-pounders and you just had the smoke effect from dropping them. So the effect of dropping bombs wasn't really apparent.

Dropping the bombs did affect the aircraft. You could feel them go, much to the relief of the rest of the crew who knew then that the job was done and to get the hell out of it.

I had no problems staying awake, and I have to admit this, until immediately after leaving the target area. I suppose that the adrenaline, the excitement and whatever took place in the approach to the target, it did require a great amount of concentration. You tried to ignore everything that was going on around you. But, as soon as we left the target and the pilot started to climb, freed from the weight of the bombs we could climb up another 5,000 feet or so, I would drop off to sleep. I had no way of stopping that and it was probably only for a very few minutes and it didn't seem to affect the crew. I never heard any complaints, they probably didn't know.

John is very clear about the success achieved by Bob Knights and his crew and their ability to return from operation after operation.

I think we remained enthusiastic all the way through. We had periods of leave every six weeks of course. We became very, very experienced, we knew what we were doing and this helped enormously, so whilst you didn't look forward to another operation, particularly over some of the targets we were assigned, you knew what you had to do so you didn't feel downhearted about it – 'Oh Lord, I wish this would be the end'. We were really concentrating on doing the number of operations we knew we had to do to get to thirty and have a rest. But when it came to the point we decided we didn't want to go that route, so I think we were in good spirits. We were reasonably satisfied with what we were doing and felt we ought to continue.

Early in 1944 John's time, and that of the rest of the crew, was up at 619 Squadron.

Hopefully, we were getting up towards becoming an experienced crew. We had gone past the danger period. However, we then had to move from Woodhall Spa to Coningsby to allow 617 Squadron to come in. We were familiar with the fact that they were going to occupy Woodhall Spa. I think we moved to Coningsby in December of '43. We did two or three more operations into January and then I think Bob must have completed his tour because we were faced with what we would be doing next. I certainly hadn't finished mine, and neither had the rest of the crew, so we would have been assigned probably to another pilot to finish our tours. We would then have gone on to a rest, instructing [at] OTUs, which we thought was going to be pretty dangerous. So we decided that we didn't really want to be split up, that the best thing to do was to stay together and thought 'how about if we joined 617 Squadron which was back down the road?' So we had a vote on it and we said 'yes we would'. I don't think the rear gunner, the mid-upper gunner and the wireless operator were all that enthusiastic but we all went along with the idea. So we asked if we could volunteer? We went for an interview with Leonard Cheshire and he asked us why we wanted to join, knowing that we were an experienced crew? So we said, 'well, we're a bit fed up with bombing at 20,000 feet, we'd like to bomb a bit lower.'

By January 1944 No. 617 Squadron was just beginning to find a role for itself. After the success of the Dams' raid the squadron had lost five crews at the Dortmund-Ems canal in September 1943 and had been searching for a way back ever since. Under the command of Leonard Cheshire a new plan was emerging of a squadron working alone, marking its own vital targets and attacking them with high levels of accuracy.

When we volunteered to go to 617 we knew what they had been doing. We also knew they'd had some serious losses after the Dams' raid. We weren't quite sure, I don't think, of the method of operating until we were appraised by Leonard Cheshire of what they were hoping to do and he did change the style so whilst we knew that we would be operating at a lower level we didn't think it would be done at ground level. Also, we knew that 617 Squadron had been operating as a small striking force and was not part of Main Force. Anyway, he accepted us. That was good. The change did us good, I certainly enjoyed it much better. I enjoyed the bombing operations with 617 because they were quite different.

I think one of the other things that we thought of going to 617 was the fact that we held it in high regard. It was held in high regard because, only a few months earlier, it had woken the whole Command and everybody up about what a small striking force could do. So we were excited about it. We knew they were an elite lot and they had the best crews – no doubt about it, they were very experienced crews – we felt we were experienced and we wanted to join them. We were followed by two or three other 619 crews to 617 so there was an aura about it and I continued to bask in this aura even after I left the squadron, which we shouldn't have done, of course. I was a bit superior to the others who hadn't been on 617 Squadron, or so I felt.

We were very pleased to be accepted. We thought we were expert enough. We had survived thirty operations. All of the crew had done pretty much most of them. We knew our way around the bomber offensive and we thought we had more to offer. We had said we didn't want to be split up, that was our main thought, and here was an opportunity to do something vastly different with a squadron that we admired and wanted to get into. Their way of operating was quite different and we were led by a very good CO, Leonard Cheshire, who was very easy to get on with but very adept at getting people to know what he wanted and he led right from the front.

So here we were in a small striking force and the method of operating suited me and I am sure it suited the rest of the crew. We weren't bombing a large city. I had nothing against that form of operation except that it had its own dangers. Here we were striking at individual targets with pinpoint accuracy with a much more accurate bomb-sight which we had to make work accurately on a specific small target. The whole thing about it was fascinating and interesting right from the start.

John's next task was to learn about the new bomb-sight that was unique to 617 Squadron.

The new kit we had was the Stabilising Automatic Bomb-sight and only that squadron was equipped with it because, firstly, [of] the way you had to use it on a normal bombing run and secondly, because [of] the way it was manufactured. As I understood it, it was made by a lot of watchmakers. It was such an intricate piece of apparatus that it was technically difficult to reproduce in quantity. So our initial instruction was not in the air. We had a lot of instruction on the ground, both the pilot and I, as it was a joint operation using the bomb-sight.

Eventually we were allowed in the air. We were assigned an aeroplane and that was going to be our aeroplane for the time on the squadron. We got in the air and off we went to Wainfleet to drop some practice bombs. And I couldn't believe it. The first two bombs I dropped hit the side of the triangle. I'd never been able to do that [before] so I thought this is some piece of equipment! It couldn't be faulted. The third time round, and this shows where the co-operation between the pilot and the bomb-aimer was absolutely essential, because the pilot had an instrument which gave him some information on the attitude of the aeroplane apart from all the other instruments and he detected that it wasn't quite right. I, as the bomb-aimer, overrode him and said no, it looks alright to me and we dropped the bomb. Of course, it was some yards off the target, so that brought it home to us how important it was to co-operate closely and both of us had to be absolutely aware that we were both on the same wavelength, [that] we agreed on the proper bombing run – lovely piece of kit.

The bomb-sight was gyroscopically controlled. Having pre-set a lot of other information on the bomb-sight itself, the characteristics of each bomb were fed into the control of the bomb-sight. The pilot had to keep the aircraft within fifty feet of the height that had been set on the bomb-sight and speed had to be absolutely accurate, so he was maintaining his position and this was a very long run, something of the order approaching five minutes bombing run into the target. Provided that the cross remained on the target it automatically followed the target as the aircraft flew along it and, at the appropriate moment determined by the information that had been put into the bomb-sight, the bomb automatically released. Now, if during the bombing run you could see some slippage where you drifted off you could have that corrected by the pilot who had his instrument. So it was close co-operation between the pilot and the bomb-aimer and being familiar with every aspect of the bomb-sight you were operating.

That was very, very good for us because it was our first operation with them and here we were attacking a small aero-engine works in France. Cheshire did the marking, dropping the flares on the target. He flew over the target a couple of times so all the workers got out and then we bombed it.

This was the 8 February 1944 attack on the Gnome-Rhône aero-engine factory in Limoges, almost 350 kilometres south of Paris. It was lightly defended as the proximity of French workers and their houses made the Germans believe it would never be attacked. Cheshire, leading 617 Squadron in his Lancaster, buzzed the factory three times before dropping incendiaries as markers from barely fifty feet. This warned the French workers to get out. The factory was destroyed and not a single French worker was killed.

The operating frequency on 617 of course was different from Main Force and I think the main reason for that was that we could only operate on moonlight nights when we could see the target. We couldn't operate over cloud because it's not possible to bomb through cloud and we were bombing at around 14,000 to 16,000 feet and so cloud was a problem. Not like with Main Force where you had target indicators and different degrees of navigation to get you to the right target. We couldn't do that on 617.

I think one of the things we really enjoyed about being on the squadron with 617 was being able to bomb accurately without too much anti-aircraft hindrance or fighters.

In the early months of 1944 the surviving crews from the Dams raid were still operating at 617 Squadron. Their presence and experience provided support to the newer crews.

The personnel on the squadron included a lot of the Dams raid people, and pilots we knew and you looked up to them for their experience. They'd been through a hell of an operation and survived and they were still operating well with the squadron so they were the leading group and you tend to emulate them as much as possible.

By the spring of 1944 No. 617 had a full schedule of operations but just as the build up for the invasion of Europe was gathering pace the crews were all stood down from operations.

The one, I suppose, disappointing thing that occurred to the squadron was that we were taken off operations early in May. We then had to undergo a lot of very intricate navigation exercises. It all looked a bit peculiar but it all became clear when, on the evening before D Day, we were assigned to carry out this operation which involved, I think, two squadrons.

This was Operation TAXABLE, part of the intricate deception plan designed to throw the Germans off the scent of the real D-Day operations.

On the operation itself it was a matter of flying over the Channel towards part of the coast near le Havre. We flew along a course that had to be accurately measured in so many seconds and then do a Rate-one turn along a parallel course and this was several aircraft flying together, along a parallel course and then join, and then take another Rate-one turn and join the original course farther [from] or nearer to the coast. In other words, we were doing a series of loops working nearer and nearer to the coast. The same time we were dropping 'Window' in different-sized bundles. The larger ones were first and as we got nearer the coast we dropped smaller ones. Again, a timed drop. There was a man with a stopwatch and a man picking up the 'Window' and stuffing it down the flare chute. This was designed to confuse the German radars on the coast at that time and made it appear as though there was an approaching naval force. And it did work. It seemed a bit odd to us but it worked. For a month we practised this routine till we had it down to a fine art. Then on the night of D Day, the night before, during the night we carried out this operation.

The report afterwards said that it worked and delayed the movement of the German forces to the west since they thought the main attack was coming near le Havre. So it worked in that respect. Strange operation.

My role was dropping 'Window' out the back end of the aircraft. There were two pilots and two navigators. There were three or four other crew on board and at a particular interval the pilots would change over. The navigators would change over and, because it was a very intricate operation, it had to be done within seconds of the turns and the turns had to be accurate and the dropping of the 'Window' was precise to the stopwatch and to the size of the 'Window' going out. It was quite a tiring operation, more so for the pilot I should think. My part was just dropping 'Window'.

Barnes Wallis had not rested after his creation of the bouncing bomb used on the Dams raid. One of his original ideas for breaking the dams had been a type of earthquake bomb that would penetrate the earth and explode deep below the surface, bringing down the structure above. He now turned his attention back to this bomb. The production Tallboy bomb was a masterpiece of engineering. Weighing five tons it was made from a single piece of steel for strength so that the bomb could survive impact with the ground. It was almost 6.5 metres long but less than a metre in diameter and its terminal velocity was faster than the speed of sound. The Tallboys were first used on the night of 8/9 June 1944.

After D Day we were pleased to get back on the bombing trail again. This time we were armed with a new weapon, the Tallboy. Very exciting. The operation three days after D Day was against the Saumur tunnel. It proved very accurate, they dropped all around the entrance to the tunnel and one on the top [and] so completely destroyed the tunnel. It proved the effectiveness of that particular weapon as it was designed to do deep penetration.

The Tallboy, when it was introduced, looked good, it looked like a bomb. I mean the dreadful 12,000-pound light case was awful, so here we had a new weapon. We couldn't practise bombing with it, but we had to know something about it and its characteristics and so forth.

Here we were, excitedly dropping the new one to see how it performed. Firstly, when it went the aircraft jumped up in the air, so you knew you'd dropped 12,000 pounds of weight. Secondly, you could follow it all the way down to the target and see where it impacted. It was designed for deep penetration; penetrate the earth with a delayed action fuse – only half second delay. It doesn't sound much but the bomb had gone in a long way because it was travelling beyond the speed of sound [and] so it was going down pretty fast. It buried [itself] and it then destroyed the foundations, which was what Barnes Wallis was after. It didn't matter if you didn't hit the target directly. As long as you put it alongside you were doing just as much damage as was intended.

Cheshire said he didn't want them dropped all over France. They were expensive and took a long time to make, so bring them back, which sounded a bit hairy at first till you realised you could land her with a 12,000-pounder on board.

After that we seemed to operate mainly in daylight as far as I recall. We hadn't done any daylight raids on Main Force. They were all night raids so here we were in daylight – that was good. So we didn't have to wait for moonlight or other conditions, provided there was no cloud over the target – that was the delaying factor that happened on a number of occasions – we had to bring the bomb back.

The bombing operations were quite different from there on, after D Day. They were involved with V-1 and V-2 weapon sites and that sort of storage site and other things. It was quite different, much better operating in daylight; the only thing was the enemy could see you as well. We started to lose one or two aircraft and anti-aircraft fire was a bit of a problem, particularly over the U-boat pens, Brest, le Havre. There was fighter activity, so you had that to contend with that as well.

I remember after D Day, June, July time, some of the older members who'd been with the squadron started to leave. The CO changed and we had James Tait, known as 'Willie'. He didn't like being known as 'Willie' but he did sign his name as 'Willie' so it must have attracted him. He took over from Cheshire; he had a different attitude. He was laid back but the squadron progressed and there were changes. But I also knew that I wasn't going to be there that much longer because I thought that my second tour should be coming up soon, I'd completed fifty, and I thought I ought to be retiring soon to do something else. You started to think the chances of survival were becoming fewer. People had been lost and we had aircraft shot down so you had to think about things like that.

I was disappointed but I felt I ought to go, mainly because I was engaged to be married. She worked in the Intelligence Section; she had thoughts on the dangers of continuing flying, even though it wasn't the same as in Main Force. The main thing that I felt quite sad about was leaving the crew. I'd been with them since March the previous year, well most of them anyway, and I felt I was leaving a family behind. It took a long time to adjust but I did get back to the squadron briefly from the OTU. My bombing leader at the OTU said he was visiting 617 and would I like to go with him so I said 'yes please'. So, of course, I went back and saw them all again during the time that they were bombing the *Tirpitz*. Wish I'd been on those.

At the same time as I left, of course, there were one or two other thoughts going on in the crew. The pilot, Bob Knights, continued, so did the rear gunner. In fact the rear gunner stayed on after the war for a short while. The navigator: I think he decided that year to pull out and he went back to Canada. But, of course, we'd had new gunners by then, so the crew had changed; there were new people coming in.

When I look back I didn't think at the time that I'd suffered. I mean you talk about post-traumatic stress disorder now, but I don't think that's what I had suffered with but I certainly noticed the difference. When I left the squadron my discipline wasn't very good, similar to the discipline of many ex-aircrew. The way that we operated during most of the free time we had, we did what we wanted.

Then, going to OTU instructing, I felt the same sort of attitude obviously didn't go down well. I was at OTU from September right through until May when it all finished. I didn't care for it very much. It was flying as I found before when I was on OTU under instruction myself. We were flying in Wellingtons which were past their best. You were with crews who were learning to fly and there were crashes but I just went through it. During that time they sent us on what was called an Air Force Officers' School, a course at Hereford where we had to learn about air force law and discipline and marching, all under the leadership of a corporal which set us back a bit. Here we were, flyers of the Air Force being told to march around and to pull ourselves together. I think that did us a bit of good.

After that, after some short while, I was sent to Catterick for re-assessment along with other air crew. Then from there I finished up, strangely, in Fighter Command down at Tangmere. And that was quite an eye opener, quite different – Fighter Command from Bomber Command. I liked it. I thought it was good. I had to become accustomed to a peacetime service. Wondering how I was going to extend my service because by then I was married and had a family and what do I do? How do I get used to being non-aircrew, as I wasn't then? Do I want to go back to the City? No, I didn't want to go back to the City. So I applied for and was given a short service commission, four years, so that started me on the road to full time in the RAF after the war.'

Looking back at all my flying time when I was now an accountant officer I tried to hang on to the image of it to some extent. So, whilst I was doing a job in accounts, which was alright, I was getting by on the fact that I found I was quite helpful to the aircrew because I'd learnt how to fill in travelling claims and also [knew] a little bit about income tax, so they used to bring their problems to me. So that was helpful, but I still considered myself as aircrew on the ground. I wore my badges and I even carried my aircrew whistle on my battle-dress until the CO said it was about time I took it down. I hung on to that image and it was some years before I had a clean break from it. But I always had that feeling of being part of aircrew now on the ground. So, I look back on it with a great amount of, well I enjoyed what I did, and felt very lucky to have survived.

At the time of writing John Bell is retired, gets involved with the 617 Squadron Association and spends much of his time raising money for the Bomber Command Memorial appeal.

Pilot Officer John Bell – Operations at 617 Squadron

- 8 February 1944 – Limoges – Gnome-Rhône aero-engine factory. The first official operation where 617 Squadron marked its own target. After three low-level passes by Leonard Cheshire to ensure French workers got out, the factory suffered massive damage with hardly any French casualties.
- 12 February 1944 – Antheor Viaduct – Near misses but viaduct hardly damaged.
- 2 March 1944 – Albert – Aircraft factory. Very successful operation with the factory being virtually destroyed.
- 4 March 1944 – St Étienne – la Ricamerie needle-bearing factory. Operation abandoned as target was not located due to cloud.
- 10 March 1944 – St Étienne – la Ricamerie needle-bearing factory. Operation only partially successful as target only slightly damaged. Many of the markers bounced off the factory.
- 15 March 1944 – Woippy – Aero-engine factory. Operation abandoned as target obscured by cloud.
- 16 March 1944 – Clermont-Ferrand – Michelin tyre factory. Very successful precision raid. Leonard Cheshire flew over the factory three times to warn French workers. Target destroyed.
- 18 March 1944 – Bergerac – Explosives factory. Factory completely destroyed.
- 29 March 1944 – Lyons – Aero engine factory. Accurate bombing. Target severely damaged.
- 10 April 1944 – St Cyr – Signals depot. Very successful operation. Target destroyed.
- 18 April 1944 – Juvisy – Marshalling yards. 617 Squadron acted as markers for 5 Group. Target destroyed

- 24 April 1944 – Munich – 617 Squadron again provided part of the marking force for Main Force. Bombing was accurate and the operation successful.
- 5 June 1944 – Operation TAXABLE – 617 Squadron flew very accurate runs towards the French coast dropping Window to simulate an allied convoy approaching. Totally successful, the operation helped to keep German forces away from the real invasion area.
- 8 June 1944 – Saumur – Railway tunnel. The first use of the Tallboy 12,000lb 'earthquake' bomb. Target destroyed, stopping many German reserves being brought to the Normandy front by rail.
- 14 June 1944 – le Havre – E-boat pens. Carried out in daylight, the raid proved that the Tallboy bombs could penetrate the massively thick concrete shelters which the Germans thought to be bomb-proof.
- 15 June 1944 – Boulogne – E-boat pens. Not as successful as the previous night's raid as many of the aircraft brought back their bombs but still much damage was caused.
- 19 June 1944 – Watten – V-2 rocket facility. Massive concrete-covered storehouse attacked but heavy cloud meant that bombing was inaccurate.
- 20 June 1944 – Wizernes – V-2 weapons site. Aircraft recalled due to cloud over the target.
- 24 June 1944 – Wizernes – V-2 weapons site. This time the squadron found and bombed the target, a storage facility being built for V2 rockets. The site was put out of use.
- 25 June 1944 – Siracourt – Flying-bomb storage facility. Target successfully attacked. 617 Squadron CO marked the target using a Mustang he had never flown before.
- 17 July 1944 – Wizernes – V-2 construction site. Another huge concrete facility to both store and launch rockets was attacked. Near misses undermined the network of tunnels, caused land slippage but left the huge concrete dome undamaged.
- 20 July 1944 – Wizernes – V-2 construction site. Unsuccessful operation. Target under cloud. Sortie abandoned.
- 25 July 1944 – Watten – V-2 construction site. Fifteen Tallboys dropped. Near misses caused huge craters and violent shaking of the structure. Bunker was abandoned.

- 31 July 1944 – Rilly la Montagne – Railway tunnel housing flying-bomb launch site. Tallboys caved in both ends of the tunnel.
- 1 August 1944 – Siracourt – Flying-bomb site. 617 attacked as part of a huge force of more than 750 aircraft. Only 10 per cent bombed; 617 recalled due to bad weather.
- 4 August 1944 – Étaples – Railway bridge. Hits were recorded but small 1,000lb bombs caused very little damage.
- 5 August 1944 – Brest – U-boat pens. One enormous bunker over 300m long attacked successfully. Six direct hits with Tallboys.

John Bell was posted to 123 OTU from 617squadron on 24 August 1944.

Chapter 5

Flight Lieutenant Tom Bennett

Tom Bennett was born in east London in 1919. He had no background in flying but when the time came to choose it was the Royal Air Force he joined.

> It's just that I fancied it more than the other services. I did weigh up going in the Navy but eventually I decided it was the RAF and joined up. I was part of the first national service group that were called up, or enlisted before the war and things carried on from there.
>
> Like everybody else I suppose, I wanted to be a pilot but I was too 'ham-fisted'. A bit heavy on the landings they reckoned. But I got a recommendation to become an observer as it was and that was the course that I followed.

Tom's initial training was as a wireless operator/gunner but he soon changed roles to become an observer and finally a navigator. In February 1942, while at 19 OTU at Kinloss in Scotland, Tom teamed up with his pilot, Gerry Fawke, with whom he would fly operationally for his whole wartime career.

Gerry and his crew were posted to 49 Squadron during the summer of 1942. Like so many other squadrons in Bomber Command, 49 had just received the new four-engined Lancaster.

> Gerry Fawke was an excellent pilot, there was no doubt about that, and I had no worries when I was in an aircraft flown by Gerry Fawke, whether it was a Lancaster or it was a Mosquito. We just dovetailed well together.

Flying the Lancaster Gerry led a highly rated crew and it was not long before their experience meant they were leading formations into combat. Their operational targets read like a list of all the places a bomber crew would choose not to go, with regular visits to the Ruhr

The famous photograph of Guy Gibson and his crew before setting off on the Dams raid on the evening of 16 May 1943. (© *Cody Images*)

ED825, AJ-T. George Johnson attacked the Sorpe Dam in this aircraft flown by Joe McCarthy. Seen here as converted for the Dams raid, this Lancaster was eventually lost on 10 December 1943 during an SOE re-supply operation over France. (© *Cody Images*)

An Upkeep 'bouncing bomb' attached to Guy Gibson's aircraft, AJ-G, before the Dams raid.
(© Cody Images)

King George VI inspecting photographs taken after the Dams raid with Guy Gibson and Air Commodore Whitworth, Officer Commanding RAF Scampton.
(© Cody Images)

Guy Gibson with a large aerial photograph of the Möhne Dam taken after the Dams raid.
(© Cody Images)

Grant McDonald (far right) with other Canadian and American aircrew who survived the Dams raid. (© *Cody Images*)

Survivors of the Dams raid photographed at a celebration dinner given by A.V. Roe at the Hungaria Restaurant in Regent Street, London, on 22 June 1943, the same day they had been to the Palace for the investiture. Barnes Wallis (sitting, second left) and Guy Gibson (sitting, centre front). Les Munro (standing, back row, third right). (© *Cody Images*)

617 Squadron photograph taken on 9 July 1943, a few days before Wing Commander Guy Gibson left the squadron. (© *Cody Images*)

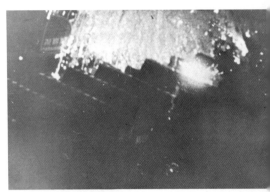

Leonard Cheshire, Officer Commanding 617 Squadron from September 1943 to July 1944. (© *Cody Images*)

Famous trio of photographs of target indicators dropped by Leonard Cheshire at very low level over the Gnome-Rhône aero-engine factory at Limoges on 8 February 1944. (© *Cody Images*)

Crater created by a 12,000lb Tallboy which destroyed the V-2 rocket site at Wizernes in France on 17 July 1944. (© *Cody Images*)

Wing Commander James Tait DSO*** DFC* who commanded 617 Squadron from July to December 1944 and led the attack that sank the *Tirpitz*. (© *Cody Images*)

Kriegsmarine photograph of *Tirpitz* in Norway. (© *Cody Images*)

A camouflaged *Tirpitz* in Altafjord, Norway. She was attacked twice by the RAF in 1944 while based there. (© *Cody Images*)

Tirpitz under attack in
September 1944.

(© *Cody Images*)

A 12,000lb Tallboy, the
type of bomb used to
sink *Tirpitz* on
12 November 1944.

(© *Cody Images*)

A direct hit scored on *Tirpitz* on 12 November 1944. (© *Cody Images*)

Tirpitz capsized after the successful attack with Tallboys on 12 November 1944. (© *Cody Images*)

The Kembs Barrage on the river Rhine near Basle. On 7 October 1944, while attacking at 600 feet, Drew Wyness' aircraft was shot down. (© *Cody Images*)

The Bielefeld Viaduct after 617 Squadron attacked with a 22,000lb Grand Slam bomb, dropped by Squadron Leader Jock Calder on 14 March 1945. (© *Cody Images*)

A Grand Slam bomb being filled with Torpex explosive at the English Steel Corporation factory in Sheffield in 1945. (© *Cody Images*)

A 22,000lb Grand Slam bomb at 617 Squadron's base at Woodhall Spa in March 1945. (© *Cody Images*)

A stunning shot of a 617 Squadron Lancaster attacking the Arbergen railway bridge on 21 March 1945. (© *Cody Images*)

(*left*) A Grand Slam bomb about to be loaded onto a 617 Squadron Lancaster in March 1945. (© *Cody Images*)

(*below*) The German island of Heligoland in the North Sea. The squadron bombed the coastal gun batteries there on 19 April 1945. (© *Cody Images*)

(*bottom*) 617 Squadron Lancasters flying over the Bavarian Alps to attack Hitler's mountain retreat at Berchtesgaden on 25 April 1945. (© *Cody Images*)

A 617 Lancaster approaching Berchtesgaden on the squadron's final bombing operation of the war. (© *Cody Images*)

Lancaster Mk VIIs of 617 Squadron over India in early 1946. This mark was flown by the squadron from June 1945 until September 1946. (© *Cody Images*)

Les Munro.
(© *Michael Jowett/Aces High Gallery, Wendover*)

Grant McDonald.
(© *Michael Jowett/Aces High Gallery, Wendover*)

George Johnson.
(© *Michael Jowett/Aces High Gallery, Wendover*)

John Bell.
(© *Michael Jowett/Aces High Gallery, Wendover*)

Tom Bennett.
(© *Michael Jowett/Aces High Gallery, Wendover*)

Frank Tilley.
(© *Michael Jowett/Aces High Gallery, Wendover*)

Benny Goodman.
(© *Michael Jowett/Aces High Gallery, Wendover*)

Murray Valentine.
(© *Michael Jowett/Aces High Gallery, Wendover*)

Murray Valentine, Benny Goodman, and John Langston.
(© *Michael Jowett/Aces High Gallery, Wendover*)

Valley and Berlin. On 17 October 1942 they took part in the famous attack on the Schneider armament factory at le Creusot over 200 miles south-east of Paris. The whole trip was flown in daylight at tree-top level. No. 49 Squadron led the attack and only a single Lancaster, from 61 Squadron, was lost. Before the end of their tours Gerry Fawke had been awarded a DFC and Tom Bennett a DFM.

Tom Bennett ended his first tour at 49 Squadron in April 1943. He spent six months in the operations room at 5 Group Headquarters before being posted to 1654 Conversion Unit at Wigsley to instruct new crews on radar navigation. Just a few miles away Gerry Fawke had been converting new Lancaster pilots on 1660 Conversion Unit at Swinderby, followed by a stint at the Lancaster Finishing School at Syerston.

At Easter 1944 Tom arrived at RAF Wyton to begin his second operational tour, this time in the Pathfinder Force. Almost immediately he got the call from Gerry Fawke.

I think the first I knew about it was Gerry Fawke was on the phone telling me to get all my gear ready and come over to Woodhall Spa because we were going to war with 617. I didn't mind and was only too pleased to think I was going back with him as we got on very well together.

In fact Gerry Fawke and Tom Bennett both had to go to 1655 Conversion Unit at RAF Warboys, near Huntingdon, to convert to flying Mosquitoes before being posted to 617 Squadron on 10 April 1944.

Gerry was the motivating force in our getting selected. He heard that Cheshire was looking for crews for his Mozzies and he flew over to Woodhall Spa and had an interview with Chesh and Chesh said I'll fix it right away and that's what happened. I think several squadrons were probably pleased. He looked at the 'Conversion' units rather than particular squadrons to supply aircrew because good aircrew were like diamonds.

Gerry and Tom immediately took to flying a Mosquito with just the two of them compared to the seven members of a Lancaster crew.

You worked close as a team. Sitting beside each other had an effect, you could communicate a lot easier, I felt. It may have meant pulling an earpiece across but, by and large, it was quite an acceptable change really. You expect it to be a bit cramped but I think you felt more in it in the Mozzie because of where you were placed as against the other aircraft.'

Tom quickly developed an idea of the workload for a navigator in a Mosquito.

You looked out for the weather, what was ahead, what was behind you. Once you were out of Gee range, looking out for pinpoints and things like that with the pilot.

The driving force behind the arrival of Mosquitoes at 617 Squadron was the squadron commander, Leonard Cheshire. He made an instant impact on Tom Bennett when he met him for the first time in the officers' mess, the Petwood Hotel, at Woodhall Spa.

It was in the Petwood itself which was our mess and I thought he was the Met Officer and then they said this is Leonard Cheshire. I thought 'Oh Christ, the bloody Met Officer'. He wouldn't disabuse people about who he was. I'm afraid we were all fans of Leonard Cheshire once you were in the squadron.

'Chesh', he was always known as 'Chesh'. It's very difficult to define because he was really the ultimate leader and he had a manner with him that drew you to him as soon as you had been in a 'do'. You got into 617 and that was it, everything went well after that.

He understood what people were going through and he could put himself in their place and he was there as a sort of defender if anything outside went wrong. Like, if the Station Commander thought something had gone wrong, 'Chesh' would think at least Gerry Fawke has been over Germany and done it all and the poor old Group Captain had just worried his way in Lincolnshire for the war.

I think he was convinced about this new method that was going to be introduced into 5 Group, so he threw his whole weight behind the move to introduce it. And, of course, there was a lot of backing up for him from the other pilots. I mean, they were no mugs and it all sort of dovetailed as 'Chesh' wanted it.

Cheshire had been frustrated by a lack of accuracy by the Path-finders on raids at the end of 1943. During one operation the bombing was so accurate that the target would have been obliterated had the markers been dropped at the right place. Cheshire took the issue into his own hands and, during an operation on 4 January 1944, he and Dams raid survivor Mick Martin dropped their own markers from low level. The markers skidded away from the target, a V-1 launch site in the Pas de Calais, so the attack wasn't quite as successful as expected but it gave Cheshire plenty to think about. Dropping markers from 400 feet in a Lancaster would test many crews, but with 617 Squadron's history it proved not to be a problem.

They kept practising and found that they had to dive-bomb to get a truly accurately dropped marker on the target. It was clear to Cheshire that, while dive-bombing in a Lancaster may be relatively easy in the hands of an experienced pilot such as Mick Martin, it would be much more dangerous for others. The answer was for the squadron to get a new aircraft, one that would allow them to mark their own targets.

No. 617 Squadron received its first Mosquitoes before the end of March with Cheshire being the first to convert. On the night of 5 April 1944 617 Squadron marked for a force of Lancasters attacking aircraft repair depots in Toulouse. These factories, owned by Bréguet and Latécoère, but utilised by the Luftwaffe during the war, were repairing damaged Heinkel He111s, Ju88s and Focke Wulf 190s. The markers were accurate and so were the bombers. The target was destroyed. Cheshire was given more aircraft and so his Mosquito marking force was created.

> There were four (Marking) teams. You would attempt to find and mark the aiming point of the target. That was the whole idea of the thing, to be low down and definitely put the markers where the Germans didn't want them. It was very interesting.
>
> The first marker fall would indicate where they thought the target was, and once you saw it you dived straight at it and released your marker as you pulled away and sent the marker on its way.
>
> Sometimes we had to mark a path going into the target. It was certainly a red spotfire, the final one, because they showed up best of all.

Within a few days of arriving at the squadron Gerry Fawke and Tom Bennett had been on their first operation.

Our first operation was on 18 April and I think they looked a bit askance at us first of all but we went in and marked and did it all satisfactorily. From then on there was a different attitude. We were in the squadron.

I remember Juvisy was an important rail junction there and the Germans were moving troops about all over the place. This was the first move to keep them in their place.

On Cheshire's first operation to Toulouse the Mosquito's speed and durability meant that he came away almost untouched by enemy flak. Tom Bennett found the same happened when he flew to Juvisy.

I think it was overemphasised, the danger, because you were travelling at a decent rate of knots by the time you got your nose down and were coming in, particularly at night time as well. And you had a good pilot so there was nothing to worry about really.'

There were three further operations during April including a major attack on Munich. It was said that Sir Arthur Harris, C-in-C of Bomber Command, had insisted that Cheshire would only get his Mosquitoes if he promised to attack Munich. True or not, the marking was accurate and massive damage was caused to Munich city centre.

Tom Bennett went on just a single trip at the beginning of May before all operations for the squadron were stopped. Training commenced for an important operation in support of D Day – Operation TAXABLE.

It was six weeks training that built you into one team. Everybody realised how important it was that this went right, otherwise it could give the whole game away. We did all the preparation well away from civilisation. It was a challenge and it was met. We did several experiments off the coast of England and ironed out whatever bugs we could that way. I think it was the realisation of what hung on it all. That you could be pointing out where the right invasion force was and that meant you had men's lives in your hands and that was quite a responsibility really.

The precision required for TAXABLE meant that even experienced navigators such as Tom Bennett needed a lot of practice.

Special attention had to be paid to setting up the Gee co-ordinates because normally, for normal navigation, you only worked to the second decimal place but for this we were dealing with yards so we had to set it to the third decimal place and you had to be bloody careful that you'd done that as well, otherwise suddenly this convoy starts doing sixty or seventy knots and even the Germans wouldn't appreciate that.

For the first time since joining 617 Squadron Tom and his pilot would not be flying in a Mosquito.

We were in Lancasters. We put a force, (a make-believe) invasion force, on the German coastwatching radar for two and a half hours. We had to keep that going and there was a changeover point which was most difficult. The relieving aircraft had to come up and do the final circuit with the last of the first wave and then we would drop down in the turn and pick the wave up again. This was the part where it could have all 'gone to the pictures' but fortunately it all went off very smoothly and TAXABLE carried on. It certainly kept the Germans in their place. We had to drop Window. Going out it was thin, thicker and thick and then coming away from the coast it had to be thick, thinner and thin. They had marshals, they called them Windowing Marshals, who made sure the right window was being dropped at the proper spot.

They didn't know (whether we succeeded or not) except for the fact that the German reaction was what we wanted but they had no more ideas than we did about the success of it, not immediately. Of course they went into it afterwards and we were patted on the back and one thing and another. When you were talking about Gee to senior officers you might as well of been talking in Chinese. No it was very much a one-man show and I was glad I was there.

After the success of Operation TAXABLE on the eve of D Day, Tom returned to his Mosquito. On 8 June 1944 he took part in the incredibly successful attack on the Saumur tunnel where the markers were dropped with pinpoint accuracy and the bombing completely blocked the tunnel, delaying reinforcements reaching the invasion area.

From then until the end of July Tom Bennett took part in many operations in support of the invasion forces. Gun batteries, E-boat and

U-boat pens and ammunition dumps were all marked and destroyed by an ever more successful 617 Squadron. In August 1944 Gerry and Tom switched to photographic sorties, following the bombers over the target and confirming the outcome of the operations.

Towards the end of June 1944 Leonard Cheshire developed his marking techniques even further. Now he decided he could dive steeper, drop markers lower and make it more difficult to be hit if he had a smaller and more manoeuvrable aircraft. On 25 June a Mustang was delivered to Woodhall Spa, uncrated and put together. Cheshire then consulted the aircraft's pilot's notes and flew it on an operation to mark a heavy concrete V-1 flying bomb store at Siracourt in the Pas de Calais. Tom Bennett remembered that Cheshire was so unfamiliar with the American controls of the Mustang that he formatted on Tom's Mosquito to get Gerry and Tom to help calibrate some of his own instruments.

On 6 July 1944, again in his Mustang, Leonard Cheshire flew his last sortie for 617 Squadron, an attack on the V-3 site at Mimoyecques, south-west of Calais and very near the French coast.

No. 617 Squadron was to have a new Commanding officer, Wing Commander James Tait, a very experienced bomber pilot who would end the war having completed over 100 operations.

> Willie (Tait) was very quiet and very sort of, I wouldn't say stand-offish, but he never had the ability to mix in the way Chesh had it. But nevertheless he was a bloody fine squadron commander.

James Tait is probably best remembered for leading 617 Squadron on three operations against the German battleship *Tirpitz*. Tom Bennett flew on the first two trips and, for the first time since TAXABLE back in June 1944, he flew with Gerry Fawke in a Lancaster.

The first operation was 11 September and rather than fly direct into the attack the squadron flew to Russia and stayed for a few days before refuelling, attacking *Tirpitz* in Alten Fjord in Norway and returning to Britain.

> When we went to Russia we were bitten to death by bugs. Some-body composed a song about the visit and that was one of the lines. 'When we went to Russia we were bitten to death by bugs.' Some worse than others. I was free of them because my family used to go hop picking in Kent so we knew a thing or two about

what could be operating in beds so we took all our gear outside in the cold and give them a good shake, all the blankets and everything, but the poor buggers who had no experience, they were almost hospital cases when they got up in the morning. Their arms were all swollen.

Two or three days I think we were there. We played football. And the Russians showed us a thing or two but we found out afterwards that they had sent this team from Moscow to make sure so whether it was the team that came over after the war that we were up against I don't know but they certainly knew their football. They even tried to teach us some Russian dancing. The weather, I wouldn't say it was ideal, bloody cold, but it was acceptable; well you were in Russia, what do you expect?

Before leaving for an operation crews would expect a detailed briefing on what was to come but in Russia it happened a little differently.

The Russians, not through any fault of theirs, weren't really contributing to what we considered was a briefing so we had to do a lot of our own digging out from sources. Compared to the way we were treated for our own operations, from UK, where you had all the maps and charts and anything you needed, you felt a bit neglected. I think they did the very best they could with lousy equipment and one thing and another and they made us very welcome. But it didn't compare with doing an operation from home.

But I think the Russians did their bloody best for us and I will always be convinced of that. I know a lot of us had to finish off in the aircraft itself with a lot of the information because the light kept going on and off in their briefing room.

Although Gerry Fawke dropped his Tallboy bomb where they assumed the *Tirpitz* was, the smokescreen thrown up around the ship stopped any real results being confirmed.

I don't remember a lot about *Tirpitz* apart from how bloody bad and big she looked. It was an important target too, especially at that time of the war for the Germans. Suddenly there was a big capital ship up there with no apparent redress. No it was just hard luck. Eventually they got in the way of a 12,000-pounder.

Attacking *Tirpitz*, with all its defences both on the ship and the shore, was a dangerous place to be.

> Christ, with 16-inch guns firing at you it's bound to be a difficult place. No, that was all part and parcel really. We expected to be fired at. They didn't put bloody brass bands out. We were only too anxious to bomb and get back again.

On 28 October Gerry Fawke took his crew back to the *Tirpitz* again. This time, however, they flew direct from Scotland rather than stopping in Russia. Tom had an extremely busy time during the long journey to and from Norway. First of all, he had to navigate the aircraft to Norway without the use of their Gee radar for the last part of the trip.

> I think you only way you could cope with that situation was to milk the Gee for all you could while you had it and then your own personal experience would help you to forecast what probably lay ahead meteorologically. After that it was definitely dead reckoning, nearer dead than reckoning I think. No it was, you eventually found yourself back in basic navigation really, flame floats and all that sort of thing. So it was a relief to get back over land and pick up a few guaranteed pinpoints.

Then he had to provide the bomb-aimer with information for the stabilised bomb sight.

> We had to do a lot of calculations for the SABS, for the bombing actually. All the bomb-aimer did was the run in and corrections and things which the semi-automatic bomb sight picked up immediately itself and as soon as it was fed in that was it. You were just waiting for 'bombs gone' and made sure he had the right course to get away on the compass.

This second trip to *Tirpitz* resulted in one hit but she was not sunk and the squadron would go back again, this time completely successfully, in November. For Tom Bennett, however, it was the end of his tour and he was posted from the squadron on 30 October 1944.

> I was pretty glad, it was probably coloured by the fact that I'd gone back to war with Gerry Fawke which to me made all the difference. I wouldn't have been particularly enamoured to have

been sent down the Pathfinder force or something like that. But if you've got somebody up the front who you've got one 110 per cent confidence in, that's one avenue you don't worry about.

Despite leaving the squadron Tom stayed at Woodhall Spa. He was appointed station navigation officer where he remained for the rest of the war. It was his time on operations and, in particular, with 617 Squadron that he remembers best.

I was always pleased I had been in Bomber Command and managed to do sixty-one trips so I felt I'd done a bit towards it anyway. I just feel that I did what I was asked to do and was glad to get away with it.

Tom Bennett stayed on in the Royal Air Force after the war, serving in Greece and the Middle East, the latter posting being back on Lancasters but this time on 38 Squadron, a maritime patrol squadron doing long-range reconnaissance and air sea rescue.

He took early retirement in 1955 when he joined the Port of London Authority. After his final retirement in 1980 Tom took an ever more active role in supporting the 617 Squadron Association, eventually becoming its archivist and writing an invaluable book about many of the characters from the squadron entitled *617 Squadron – The Dambusters at War*.

Sadly Tom Bennett passed away on 9 January 2013, the last of Leonard Cheshire's Mosquito men.

Flight Lieutenant Tom Bennett – Operations at 617 Squadron

- 18 April 1944 – Juvisy – Marshalling yards. 617 Squadron acted as markers for 5 Group. Target destroyed.
- 20 April 1944 – la Chapelle – Railway yards in the north area of Paris. Target heavily bombed. It was the first test for the new 5 Group marking method using 617 Squadron plus further 5 Group Pathfinder squadrons. Very successful operation.
- 22 April 1944 – Brunswick – First use of 5 Group's marking method over a German city. Cloud hindered the bombing of the target.
- 24 April 1944 – Munich – 617 Squadron again provided part of the marking force for Main Force. Bombing was accurate and the operation successful.

- 3 May 1944 – Mailly le Camp – German military camp in France. Four Mosquitoes from 617 marked successfully. Communications problem meant that bomber force had to circle the target and forty-two Lancasters lost.
- 5 June 1944 – Operation TAXABLE – 617 Squadron flew very accurate runs towards the French coast dropping Window to simulate an allied convoy approaching. Totally successful, the operation helped to keep German forces away from the real invasion area.
- 8 June 1944 – Saumur – Railway tunnel. The first use of the Tallboy 12,000lb 'earthquake' bomb. Target destroyed, stopping many German reserves being brought to the Normandy front by rail.
- 14 June 1944 – le Havre – E-boat pens. Carried out in daylight, the raid proved that the Tallboy bombs could penetrate the massively thick concrete shelters which the Germans thought to be bombproof.
- 20 June 1944 – Wizernes – V-2 weapons site. Bombers recalled due to cloud over the target.
- 22 June 1944 – Wizernes – V-2 weapons site. Bombers recalled due to cloud over the target.
- 24 June 1944 – Wizernes – V-2 weapons site. This time the squadron found and bombed the target, a storage facility being built for V-2 rockets. The site was put out of use.
- 25 June 1944 – Siracourt – Flying-bomb storage facility. Target successfully attacked. 617 Squadron CO marked the target using a Mustang he was flying for the first time.
- 4 July 1944 – St-Leu-d'Esserent – Flying-bomb storage in chalk caves north of Paris. Successful operation.
- 6 July 1944 – Mimoyecques – V-3 weapons site. The site was put out of use.
- 17 July 1944 – Wizernes – V-2 construction site. Another huge concrete facility to both store and launch rockets was attacked. Near misses undermined the network of tunnels and caused land slippage but left the huge concrete dome undamaged.
- 20 July 1944 – Wizernes – V-2 construction site. Unsuccessful operation. Target under cloud. Sortie abandoned.
- 25 July 1944 – Watten – V-2 construction site. Fifteen Tallboys dropped. Near misses caused huge craters and violent shaking of the structure. Bunker was abandoned.

- 5 August 1944 – Brest – U-boat pens. One enormous bunker over 300m long attacked successfully. Six direct hits with Tallboys.
- 6 August 1944 – Lorient – Keroman U-boat base. Successful operation with two hits recorded.
- 12 August 1944 – Brest – U-boat pens. Successful operation. Three hits recorded.
- 13 August 1944 – Brest – Shipping. Successful attack designed to prevent the German use of ships to block Brest harbour. French battleship *Clemenceau* sunk.
- 16 August 1944 – la Pallice – U-boat pens. Bombers recalled due to heavy cloud over the target.
- 18 August 1944 – la Pallice – U-boat pens. Successful attack.
- 24 August 1944 – Ijmuiden – E-boat pens. Successful attack.
- 27 August 1944 – Brest – Shipping. Merchant ships attacked to stop them being used to block Brest harbour. Successful operation.
- 15 September 1944 – Alten Fjord – *Tirpitz*. Crews had flown to Russia four days earlier. They now took off, flew the two hours to Alten Fjord where they bombed. One hit but it was decided further attacks were needed.
- 3 October 1944 – Westkapelle – Sea wall. Bombers brought their bombs back as an earlier raid had already breached the wall.
- 7 October 1944 – Kembs – Rhine barrage. Lock gates attacked successfully.
- 29 October 1944 – Tromso – *Tirpitz*. Target had moved closer to the UK so a direct attack was planned. Last minute change in wind direction meant heavy cloud covered target. Tallboys dropped but no hits recorded.

Tom Bennett was posted from 617 Squadron on 30 October 1944.

Chapter 6

Flight Sergeant Frank Tilley

Frank Tilley describes his decision to join the RAF as 'not terribly glamorous'. He was in a reserved occupation, working for a firm called Desoutter Brothers in Hendon which manufactured artificial limbs, but found it to be a very boring job. He found out he could not join the forces because he was in a reserved occupation. However, he learned that if he volunteered for RAF aircrew then he could be released. And that is why he went for aircrew. At the time he had the choice of which particular trade in aircrew he could apply for and it transpired that to apply for a pilot meant a very, very long wait before he was called up and so he decided to go for flight engineer because the intakes were of fairly short duration.

There were other compelling reasons why Frank joined up as well.

The impact of the news and propaganda that was coming out certainly did give you a damn good reason for volunteering. And I think for most of us there was a sense of duty perhaps but mainly, don't forget we were young in our late teens or early twenties, it was a sense of adventure and obviously it was very much glamorised by the press reports. I think really that's what triggered most of us to join up. I think it must have been early in 1943, about February time when I joined up. I remember the day.

We went to Lord's Cricket Ground to be mustered as they called it and I think there was a Test Match on which we were allowed to watch while we were waiting to be taken into the RAF with all the formalities etc.

Lord's Cricket ground in St John's Wood, London, was requisitioned as the Aircrew Receiving Centre, or ACRC, with local flats being used as billets. Between 1941 and 1944 around 150,000 RAF personnel passed through its doors on the way to war.

I spent two weeks in London, billeted in those rather luxury flats in St John's Wood. This was for the initial training like marching and getting used to the RAF, wearing uniforms and so on, before we went to what they called the Initial Training Wing which, for flight engineers, was down in Torquay. We spent about six weeks at Torquay with various aspects of RAF training. Apart from the obvious discipline training like marching and so forth you did things like dinghy drill which may have come in useful later on, elementary navigation, and RAF law which you needed to know about. There were lectures every day covering all aspects of the flying side of the RAF but not particularly technical at that stage.

We then had further training at St Athan in South Wales which was the RAF training place for flight engineers. I think the course was around six months and they started by teaching us fairly basic aircraft engineering, about the engines themselves and about magnetos and compression ratios and a little bit of electrics, lots of mechanics as it were. It was really general aircraft, the knowledge of what an aircraft actually is, how it flies, what are the control surfaces, what are they for, about the centre of gravity, that sort of flying discipline, the sort of thing you needed to know if you were going to fly an aeroplane. Whether you were a crew member or a pilot you still needed to know how an aircraft flew.

Like my friends with whom I came through these courses, we seemed to find that the Lancaster bomber was the one that we regarded as the favourite machine. You did have a sort of choice actually. At the end of the first part of your course at St Athan, you had to consider which particular aircraft you hoped to be further trained on. We were all assembled in this rather large hanger, and the officers over on the other side would call out that they needed say ten people for Sunderlands for example and there would be a mad rush to get onto Sunderlands. Those that were disappointed went back to where they were previously and they'd go onto the next aircraft. It was rather thought-provoking perhaps that the largest numbers that were required were for Lancasters, Halifaxes and Stirlings.

I put myself forward for the Lancaster straight away and there was no problem getting onto that as they were a bit short of them. There weren't too many people racing for the Hampden – or the Blenheims!

The first time a flight engineer crewed up or met his crew was at the next stage of training. You were now a competent flight engineer for the Lancaster bomber, for example. You were then transferred to a sort of finishing school where your pilot-to-be and his crew that you were about to join would be introduced to the Lancaster itself. Up until that point they would have probably been training as a crew on a twin-engined aircraft such as the Anson or the Airspeed Oxford, that sort of thing. They were now going to transfer to a four-engined bomber and this was, in my case, at a place called Syerston. That's where I met the crew, my pilot was Flying Officer Arthur Joplin from New Zealand. We weren't actually put together, it was a kind of choice if you like. It was all rather sort of casual but yes that's the way it was.

The relationship within the crew really was a hundred per cent most important. If you didn't get on then you really were in trouble. As it happened Joppy was a wonderful pilot and a wonderful captain of the aircraft. He was able to fit in with everybody and he got on well with all of us. We really felt very happy to have him as our pilot. Likewise I got on very well with Lofty the bomb-aimer and Basil the navigator and Cookie the wireless operator and so on; it was first class really, it was a damn good team. If anything went wrong with that then that could be serious.

In the air if we were on operations itself, the crew needed to communicate with each other but it was very limited, just what was necessary. The conversation between the pilot and myself was obviously during take-off, landing, approaching the target and little incidents that might happen during the flight but I think there was no extraneous conversation at all.

For the next two or three weeks we were trained to fly in four-engined Stirling bombers and it was probably the first time the pilot had flown a four-engined bomber, so he needed to be 'genned' up on that and the flight engineer would be doing the same. After the Stirling we then went on to the Lancaster training and spent a few weeks flying the Lancaster bomber. The training was interspersed with lectures by people who had perhaps finished a tour and were now coming to explain to you what you were heading into, which was perhaps a cautionary tale in lots of ways. After that you were then selected to go to a squadron.

The flight engineers had lectures and finally we had an examination, a written examination to assess our ability and by some fluke or other I happened to come out top of this particular group of flight engineers. Unbeknown to me the rest of the crew were having a similar assessment and it so happened that because we had all passed out fairly high in our respective disciplines we were selected to go to 617 Squadron. Well, we really didn't know what 617 Squadron was, we just assumed it was our next posting and, our crew together with Benny Goodman's crew who were also selected, found ourselves going to Woodhall Spa to join 617 Squadron. And that's really how it happened, how we came to go straight to 617 Squadron which we subsequently found out was a very famous squadron crewed mainly by veterans, real veterans. I always felt very humble. We were absolute sprogs coming on to this famous squadron having never flown an operation in our lives.

But we weren't embarrassed in any way by the attitude of the veterans. They welcomed us with open arms. They were very kind to us. It was 'come in and get on with it' as it were.

Sergeant Frank Tilley was posted to 617 Squadron from 51 Base on 15 August 1944. The Base was an example of a numbering system used by the RAF from the beginning of the huge Bomber Command expansion period in 1942. The 5 meant it was a 5 Group station and the 1 was the number of the base within the Group.

When we got there we were summoned to see the Commanding Officer. That was Wing Commander Willie Tait. He shook each of us by the hand individually and welcomed Joppy to the squadron with a very nice welcome and said he hoped we would be very happy there and then we were dismissed. From then on you spent quite a bit of time in your respective disciplines, so the navigators would spend it in the navigation office, the wireless operator with his group, the flight engineer with his and so on, and that was how you spent your day. Then perhaps you'd be told you were going to be trained further on a cross-country trip. There were numerous cross countries – daylight and night flights – and that's how you carried on day by day until there was an operation declared.

There were still some of the old Dambusting aircraft on the squadron and they were easily recognised by the cutaway in the bottom part of the fuselage. On one occasion as a crew, we were told to test fly one that had been under the maintenance staff and it was a joke really. We were detailed to take off for a couple of hours' air test and when we landed the ground crew presented us with a laurel wreath made of sparking plugs and bits of wire. We were congratulated for coming back alive. It was all rather jocular.

Frank Tilley took part in his first operation on 27 August 1944 as part of Arthur Joplin's crew.

Our first operation was in daylight and it was to the Brest peninsula in France so it was obviously a fairly cushy trip. We were little bit nervous, little bit apprehensive. We weren't carrying the Tallboy, we were carrying 1,000-pounders and it was to bomb certain shipping in Brest harbour. As we approached the target I became more and more nervous. I suppose you did get a bit keyed up. But we bombed and did the best we could. We weren't attacked by any fighters. There was flak and we weren't touched really. We just turned and went for home and that was the first operation over, 'done and dusted.'

After the first trip, one afternoon I was summoned to the Flight as it was called and told that I was going to have to fly with Squadron Leader Wyness that night. Well that was fine. I met his crew and they treated me like I'd always been there, they were marvellous really. They were very much a veteran crew; they knew what they were doing. I was naturally a bit nervous being with somebody like Squadron Leader Wyness but I behaved as normal, did my normal job and was accepted as his flight engineer. I shall remember the trip as long as I live. It was dreadful. It was the Dortmund-Ems Canal Aqueduct. And because it was such a hot target they timed it so we went out with Main Force who were bombing Dortmund itself. That was to give us a bit of cover from the sheer volume of aircraft. We were attacked by fighters several times approaching and leaving the target. But his crew were obviously very experienced and we managed to survive, we weren't hit as far as I know. But it was pretty hair-raising from my point of view being a sprog flyer and this being my first night operation. I can remember seeing at least eleven Lancasters shot down in flames that night and it is an image that I carry with me to this day. I've never been more glad to see

Woodhall Spa as we were that night. When we landed Squadron Leader Wyness said 'oh well done, Engineer' – called me 'engineer'. 'What was our fuel consumption?' Well heck, I told him and he said 'thank you very much' and that was that. That was my first experience of a night operation.'

This target had been the Dortmund-Ems Canal or more precisely the aqueduct which carried the canal over the river Glane north of Munster. The canal was the most important transport route between the Ruhr valley and the North Sea and as such had been identified as a prime target at the outbreak of war. Flight Lieutenant Rod Learoyd of 49 squadron had gained his VC for gallantry on an attack there in August 1940. No. 617 Squadron had attacked it twice in 1943, resulting in the loss of five Lancasters including thirteen aircrew who had survived the original Dams raid. This time the raid was successful. With 617 Squadron leading a force of 136 Lancasters and five Mosquitoes, two Tallboys created breaches in the banks of the canal, heavily disrupting the flow of raw materials to and from the factories and mines of the Ruhr valley.

Drew Wyness and his crew made four bombing runs but, with the target obscured by cloud, they brought their bomb back.

Squadron Leader Wyness had to corkscrew several times. I had no part to play in it, I mean he'd got the steering column I hadn't. I just clung on because when you dive you almost float off the floor because you don't weigh very much. Then, when he rolls and starts climbing you're crushed down. So, it was just a question of hanging on and making certain that the aircraft was behaving properly. But you didn't have any real part to play in a corkscrew. It was gunners and the pilot.'

As a flight engineer Frank Tilley had a vital role to play before and throughout an operation.

Pre-flight activities of a flight engineer was to liaise with the ground crew who, poor devils, spent their lives out on these wintry dispersals keeping the aircraft maintained and it was the duty of the flight engineer to be in touch with these guys to ensure that everything about the aircraft was all a hundred per cent. You arrived at the aircraft for your operation from the crew bus which carted you round and the crew loaded themselves into the aircraft to their respective stations. My job as flight engineer was to make certain that the door was closed, make my way up to the cockpit and stand alongside the pilot as we started the engines in co-operation with the ground crew. Then I did some pre-flight checks on the engines to ensure that the magnetos were working a hundred per cent and certain things one had to do. Another thing you did was we revved the engines to a certain rpm before letting them idle again.

Having got the engines warmed up and checked we were ready, you told the ground crew to take the chocks away and the pilot would then taxi the aircraft out to the take-off point which was just by the so called 'caravan'. These were the guys who ensured that the runways were cleared for taking off. When they gave you a green from the Aldis lamp you taxied onto the runway, the pilot lined everything up and we then took off. Take off was around about a 100 knots. And once the aircraft was lifted the pilot would say to me 'wheels up' and I would operate the lever which would raise the undercarriage. At this point I should point out that I would have already lowered the flaps to take off angle – I think it was fifteen degrees. Once the aircraft was airborne and the pilot was happy he would ask me to raise the flaps and this I would do with the lever. We were now in a perfect trim for flying and after the appropriate speed had been reached the pilot would ask me to reduce the revs to cruising, which was something like 2,850 rpm. We would be flying and climbing usually to operational height or whatever the height was for that particular operation. Once I'd done that it was a question of just setting, making sure that the engines were running sweetly. I would do checks on the temperature, pressures and in fact every aspect of the flying side of the aircraft. Every half an hour I would make an entry into the flight engineer's log which gave the time the readings from the various dials including the fuel state and although one didn't necessarily rely on the gauges for the fuel state they were fairly accurate, we still did a calculation which was based upon the boost settings the rev settings and the duration and that told me how to work out the fuel consumption. This was done every half an hour.'

It was this precision and accuracy that allowed bombers to fly long distances to targets and still have enough fuel to get them home.

Probably the best example of this for Frank Tilley was the trip on 12 November 1944 when the great German battleship, *Tirpitz*, was sunk.

I can remember this very vividly. We rendezvoused in Norway having flown up the length of Sweden with the rest of the squadron. When one considers that we navigated all that way on dead reckoning, we all arrived within about ten minutes of each other and the whole squadron was circling over this lake. Then a Very cartridge was fired from the Wing Commander's aircraft which meant that we had to follow him. So we formed up into what we called a gaggle and headed for the target which was less than a hundred miles away. When we got to the actual fjord we instantly saw the *Tirpitz* sitting there some thirty miles ahead. The rest of the squadron I think had probably been instructed to bomb from a certain direction and they veered off to prepare for that manoeuvre. Our bomb-aimer advised Joppy our pilot that he'd much prefer to home in on the *Tirpitz* as he saw it there and then because it was sitting there in the blue sky, beautiful clear morning, absolutely wonderful. The bomb-sight we used was the Stabilised Automatic Bomb Sight. It was quite clever really. The bomb aimer peered through an illuminated graticule and by moving various controls left, right and up and down he could arrange the graticule so that it was precisely centred on the *Tirpitz*. As we approached the *Tirpitz* the graticule moved with the aircraft. The bomb-aimer's job was to keep that control and the servo running at the right speed so that it centred itself on the *Tirpitz* the whole time. Now if the aircraft wandered left or right the bomb-aimer would correct this by keeping the graticule on the target and that sent a signal to the pilot who had a couple of indicators on the cockpit right in front of his eyes, left and right. His job was to keep those two indicator pointers dead centre. And this is the way you did it minute after minute keeping everything dead right. My job as flight engineer was to keep the flying speed absolutely precise. I think it was 180 knots and also to ensure that the altitude was constant as well. As we got farther along the bombing run, the people on the ground gave us a pretty hot reception. The flak was coming up thick and fast, including flak from the actual guns on the *Tirpitz* itself. It seemed to be getting closer and closer. The bomb-sight released the bomb automatically. When the bomb went you felt a little jerk as the aircraft was relieved of this five and a half tons of weight. You then kept on this track while the camera recorded your bomb. After that you closed the bomb doors. That stopped the camera running and we dived away out of all this flak down to sea level to make our way home. We had a brief look at the *Tirpitz* which was by now shrouded in smoke and we dived away. When we got down to sea level, making our way home, my job was to shut down the throttles for maximum fuel economy. I closed the throttles down to zero boost or something like minus two or three boost. To my horror the port outer engine wasn't responding. It was sitting there running at plus-seven boost. This would have an effect on our fuel consumption so I had to do some calculations and I recommended to Joppy that we leave the port outer running at plus-seven and feather the port inner hoping that would balance the aircraft as best we could, which it more or less did. After about five and a half hours of flying at a thousand feet above the sea we were now approaching the UK again. I was worried about the fuel states. We were certainly very low on fuel so I recommended that we land at the Shetlands. We asked permission to land at the Shetlands which was really a Coastal Command airfield equipped for dealing with flying boats, Sunderlands and such like. The runway was very short and at the end of the runway was a small mountain. We approached there, having feathered the port outer and started up the port inner, we now had got three engines under control. The pilot made an attempt at landing, but as he came in a bit high we overshot and went round again. On the second attempt he made a jolly good landing on three engines. We were greeted by the ground staff with coffee and sandwiches which was very nice and they told us they'd heard the news report that we had actually sunk the *Tirpitz*. While all this was going on I approached the ground maintenance people and being a Coastal Command crew they were not equipped with the high trestles for reaching the engines of a Lancaster, so I borrowed a ladder. I took the cowling off the port outer and there was this control link that had come adrift. So I managed to fasten it back and got Joppy to sit in the pilot's seat and operate the throttle and it was working beautifully. We closed the cowling, gave the ladder back and when we were ready we started up the engines on the aircraft batteries and we took off to make our way home which we did uneventfully.

Of course the age and hours flown by the aircraft were critical to the efficiency of its engines. Despite the quality and regularity of servicing, age took its toll. Inside the aircraft, operating conditions and material comforts were sparse for the young aircrew.

> The aircraft was a pretty old one. We weren't surprised because, after all, we were a sprog crew and I think we just accepted it and I have to say that it wasn't a terribly efficient aircraft as far as fuel consumption was concerned. It was very cramped in the aircraft but it wasn't cold because you had heating. It was smelly because of all the fuel, the horrible smell of hundred octane. And you didn't have much to eat. You had some nuts and raisins and perhaps a bar of chocolate or something. I'm not sure but I don't think we had anything to drink. We never had an issue of thermos flasks or anything. So yeah, we were pretty hungry for thirteen and a half hours. You had a meal before you set off and another one when you came back and that was all.
>
> At night, obviously, you couldn't see anything unless something was happening around you like an aircraft being shot at or in flames. There was very little you could see until you approached the target and I suppose it depended on what the target was. You could see the bombing markers if they were appropriate. At the Dortmund-Ems Canal I don't really remember seeing any markers, I think it was dead sight on by the bomb-aimer on to the aqueduct. I know we broke it but that's about all I can tell you on that one. But regarding generally what you saw, in daylight you were just scanning the sky the whole time unless you were doing a job on the gauges. To my right there was what they called a blister in the Perspex and I could actually put my head in there and look below or forward. On the *Tirpitz* trip when Lofty the bomb-aimer was doing his job on the bomb-sight, he said 'there's flak coming up Joppy, flak coming up'. And so I looked out and he was right; you could see these pretty coloured shells coming up. They seemed to come up so slowly. It would be yellow ones and red ones and black ones, grey ones. You could actually almost feel you could touch them. You felt sort of 'Gosh, I wonder if that's got my name on it'. You could actually see these shells coming up, but you'd only see them in daylight, at night no way. And of course when they burst all you saw was a big puff of smoke.

The only tracer I remember was on the flight with Squadron Leader Wyness. That was a night flight. When we were attacked this tracer just swept across the top of the aircraft, missing us fortunately. But you could imagine what'd be like if you got hit. But it was just bright white streaks of light.

On 7 October Frank flew on his fourth operation, a trip to attack the Kembs barrage on the Rhine north of Basle. He has deep misgivings about the tactics for that operation and, in particular, the low level flying.

They fitted, I think, five or six aircraft to fly low level with this special bomb-sight and they had several of those training with this sight. I'm not quite sure who went in first, whether it was the low-level lot or us. The idea was that these people would be flying in at about 600 feet. Now 600 feet along a well-armed river is madness in my opinion because – 600 feet, that's ideal for a machine gunner I would think, and it's amazing they didn't lose the lot. Anyway that's what they did with time delay bombs, Tallboys. Wing Commander Tait went first and going in first he got the element of surprise, he went straight through. I'm not quite sure what happened to the others but I think near the end of the low-attack Squadron Leader Wyness went in and he got shot up and he ditched in the Rhine. Apparently the crew were still alive and the aircraft floated. The dinghy deployed itself; they jumped in the dinghy and tried to paddle presumably towards the Swiss border. But they were arrested by German troops and I found out years and years after that they were all murdered in cold blood and nobody has ever been accounted for it.'

Drew Wyness had been at 617 Squadron since August 1944 after being posted from 57 Squadron. Like Frank Tilley the Kembs barrage trip was just his fourth for 617 Squadron. It seems that he and his crew were captured after they ditched and at least four of them were taken by 'Nazi party officials' and shot in the back of the head. The other three vanished without trace and it is suspected that the same fate befell them.

However the crew's finest hour had been the attack on *Tirpitz* on 12 November 1944. It was a daunting operation. The *Tirpitz* had been public enemy number one since the outbreak of war along with her sister ship, *Bismarck*, because of their sheer size and firepower. It was certain that they would cause havoc with a lightly defended convoy working its way across the Atlantic bringing vital supplies from the USA. *Bismarck* had been sunk in 1941 but not before her tremendous armament had sunk HMS *Hood*, the pride of the Royal Navy. That showed the potential danger to Allied shipping should *Tirpitz* ever leave her home waters. As it happened *Tirpitz* spent her war moving from one Norwegian fjord to another. Hitler had assumed that any invasion of German-occupied Europe would happen in Norway; *Tirpitz* was expected at various times to leave her harbour and attack the Russian convoys; and a constant series of attacks from both RAF and Naval aircraft as well as submarines and 'chariots', the human torpedoes, kept her in her lair. However the threat remained.

Although many previous attacks had damaged *Tirpitz* the invention of the Tallboy finally saw a weapon that was capable of sinking her once and for all. No. 617 Squadron, together with 9 Squadron, under-took three separate attacks during September, October and, finally, November 1944.

The Tallboy weighed five-and-a-half tons, I suppose, but for a fine aircraft like the Lancaster, it really didn't make any difference. On the *Tirpitz* trip since the aircraft were loaded up with extra fuel tanks we were well above the all-up weight as specified by the manufacturer. The tyres were pretty flat and the actual take off was pretty hazardous, I mean we just about got airborne from Milltown over the sea. But apart from that once the aircraft was airborne, wheels were up and the flaps retracted there was very little difference whether you had a bomb on board or not. The aircraft manoeuvred quite happily.

For the last (*Tirpitz*) trip the briefing was slightly different to the previous one in that between the second trip and the final trip the Germans had brought down a couple of squadrons of fighters to be near the *Tirpitz*. That naturally added to our apprehension. But as it happened the fighters didn't turn up.

After the sinking of *Tirpitz* Heinrich Ehrler, the commander of III/JG5, the fighter squadron which had been moved into the area to help protect *Tirpitz* from air attack, was court martialled, found guilty and demoted. However it seems to have been a communication prob-lem between the Luftwaffe and the German Kriegsmarine. Already airborne, the fighters were given conflicting information and were too late to attack the RAF Lancasters. Later in the war Ehrler's rank was restored before he was sent to fly Me262 jet fighters in Germany. Early in April 1945 he was killed ramming an American B-24 Liberator, having already shot down two other US bombers.

The object was to reduce weight as much as possible but, having said that, the weight was increased by two extra tanks. There was a long rectangular tank from a Wellington and on top of that was one of these rather contoured tanks from a Mosquito. They were connected together with a series of pipes and it was my job to cross balance the fuel. Now, to reduce weight as far as possible they removed the mid-upper turret. I think they took the guns out of the front turret and the ammunition for the four guns in the rear turret was reduced to something like 500 rounds, as far as I was told. I think the other thing they did was remove the armour plate which was normally behind the seat of the pilot. To give the aircraft enough power to take off with all this weight, they changed the engines to Merlin Twenty-fours which were the most powerful Merlins at that time, I understand, and they fitted paddle bladed props to give extra thrust.

We were briefed at Woodhall Spa and then we flew from Woodhall Spa to Milltown or Lossiemouth, we were allocated Milltown where we left the aircraft. We were then taken by transport to Lossiemouth which was the main aerodrome and we spent the night at Lossiemouth. I remember we went out in the evening to Lossiemouth village or town centre. We went to a dance in all our flying gear. We had great big flying-boots on but we had a nice evening chatting up the girls in Lossiemouth. Then the following day we were briefed again and this is when we were told about the fighters that had been brought down to Norway to defend the *Tirpitz*. And after the briefing we were then sent off to our respective aircraft. So we were taken by transport back to Milltown, and we got to our aircraft, got everything ready and we took off about three am on the twelfth of November.

The conditions up there were pretty dreadful. It was freezing. The aircraft had to have their wings sprayed with de-icing fluid because we were in danger of icing up. It was pitch dark, there was no moon. I mean, conditions weren't really very nice. I think Milltown just had one runway. We taxied onto the runway and were ready for take-off. We were given the green Very light and off we went and roared off down the runway which just terminated at the edge of the water. It was a question of take-off or swim. But we did lurch into the air as far as I can remember and once we were airborne, we were OK, we were happy.

After take-off we were detailed to fly at 1,000 feet in order to get below the German radar and headed out past the Shetlands. At around about that time the Gee Box was unable to give you any information, so that meant the electronic navigation was no longer available. From then on the navigator had to use dead reckoning. This involved taking astro shots from the astrodome on the stars and getting wind drift by means of taking a shot on a flame float that was thrown out by me through the door. I would tell the rear gunner that I'd just dropped the flame float and once he'd spotted it he would direct his gun sight onto the flame float and then relay that reading to the navigator, meaning so many degrees east or west. The navigator would then use that as part of his calculations. After I don't know how long, perhaps an hour or so, we then headed east and climbed to about 7,000 feet because we were heading for the Norwegian mountains. We flew over the top of the mountains and they looked very picturesque in all their snow, headed across Norway into Sweden and then headed north. The Swedes threw up some anti-aircraft fire on occasions but not in our particular direction and we flew up Sweden until we headed for our rendezvous point which was at this this big lake. The rest of the squadron were already there. After circling for a few minutes Wing Commander Tait fired off Very cartridges, which was our signal to follow the squadron to the target.

The best I can tell you is that the early bombs seemed to be dead on target to me. I always maintain that our own bomb release, there was nothing wrong with it. If that bomb-sight was working properly we wouldn't have been far off because I can vouch for the fact that our air speed was dead right, our height was dead right, all the graticules in the cockpit were right, so that bomb would have been fairly close. You can't tell from the photograph because all you see is lots of smoke.

Part of the training was what to do if that happened if you baled out or crash landed or something. You had to evade capture. It was ingrained into you so that you thought 'gosh I mustn't be captured'. I think if I'd have been shot down I'd have done everything I could to get away. We had compasses concealed in our boots and handkerchiefs that were really maps and all this sort of thing. On the way to the target there was the feeling of anticipation and you were really keyed up because you had to do everything right. So the time seemed to go very quickly especially as on the way up to the *Tirpitz* we were largely flying more across land than on the way back. So there wasn't any chance of getting bored, no way. In any case I was doing flame float stuff first of all. Then there was a question of keeping your eye on everything regards altitude, looking out for any trouble from enemy fighters or anything like that. So on the way up you felt very busy all the time. After we'd bombed and we came away on the first trip, where we hadn't got engine trouble or anything, the aircraft was behaving normally. It did seem a long six hours or so, flying down at sea level almost for all that time. You passed the time by chatting away there. I remember I went down to the bomb-aimer's department for a change and Lofty came up and sat where I normally would be.

The following day the squadron was lined up with 9 Squadron for a ceremonial welcome from Sir Archibald Sinclair from the Air Ministry and he congratulated us and we were given thirty-six hours' leave. Basil my navigator and I were sort of mates really, more than perhaps with the others but we went to London and saw a show, Tommy Trinder at the Palladium I think it was and he cracked a joke about the *Tirpitz* on the stage, funnily enough.

On 8 December 1944 Arthur Joplin and his crew were one of nineteen aircraft from 617 Squadron to be sent to bomb the Urft Dam, some fifty miles south west of Cologne in the Eifel National Park. The raid as a whole was unsuccessful despite over 200 Lancasters from 5 Group being sent on the raid. What this and a subsequent raid perhaps proved was that the Tallboy was less successful when used against dams than the original Upkeep bouncing bomb had been but, by this period of the war, there were no Upkeeps available, no Lancasters modified to fly them and no crews trained to drop them. This operation was a difficult one for Frank Tilley.

We did get hit by flak on the Urft dam. We were flying at about 7,000 feet then. We were on our bombing run and we didn't drop our bomb because the dam had already been breached and since these bombs were expensive we brought it home. As we turned away from the target we got struck underneath by flak, probably from a Bofors gun. The first thing I knew about it was the cockpit was full of what I thought was smoke. We thought we were on fire so we grabbed a fire extinguisher and then realised it wasn't smoke, it was hydraulic fluid that was being atomised by the terrific air pressure forcing it into the aircraft. And so that was all our hydraulic fluid gone. So it was rather fortunate that we hadn't dropped our bomb because the bomb acted as a shield, bullet-proof, or flak-proof shield because the flak would have come straight through the floor otherwise but it just bounced off the bomb and punctured these hydraulic pipes on its way out I suppose. So we had to fly back without any hydraulics. We were diverted due to fog to Manston (Kent). Manston was a crash 'drome which had a FIDO [Fog, Intensive Dispersal Of] installation. FIDO was where they burned fuel either side of the runway. You were confronted with two rows of flames either side of the runway which effectively lifted the fog. The pilot flew into this tunnel, apparently of clear air but it was quite spectacular. It was like flying into hell because it was just flames. As we had no hydraulics the way to lower the undercarriage was by means of an emergency bottle of highly compressed air. This lowered the wheels alright, but once they were down you couldn't bring them back up again. I looked out of the starboard window at the right hand undercarriage wheel and realised it was punctured because the slipstream was pressing the tyre almost flat. So I told Joppy he'd have to land on one wheel. We had to lower the flaps by emergency air as well and made a fairly good landing on one wheel, holding the aircraft up at a peculiar angle until the airspeed dropped so much that the aircraft finally settled down. It did a sort of ground loop, it swivelled round but no worse than that. And we stopped quite safely. When we got the aircraft out of the way, Wing Commander Tait was waiting for us because we were obviously a bit late; the rest of the squadron had already landed. And that was the end of that little operation. We got away with it scot free.

An even bigger force of Lancasters was sent to attack the Urft Dam again three days later. Using a different aircraft Arthur Joplin and his crew went again. This time some hits were scored on the dam but again no breach was made.

> OK, 617 was a brilliant squadron, I mean I think it was far and above anything else that happened during the war as regards bombing accuracy was concerned, it was very, very good. But it doesn't alter the fact that they got all the credit for everything in most of the war and these poor old Main Force people losing dozens and dozens of aircraft night after night and very unsung really. And I think it's pretty sad, I've always felt that. I remember going on leave soon after I joined the squadron, I think I'd done five trips and I went on leave and I met a flight engineer named Harry Odes who was on the same training course as myself and he was on Main Force. And he said to me 'how many trips have you done?' and I said 'Five'. He said, 'you lucky blighter, I've nearly finished my tour', but he was a nervous wreck. He said 'if I get through this, you know, I shall pray with thanks.'

Frank Tilley will always remember 21 December but not for the right reasons. The target was the synthetic oil refinery at Politz. His was one of sixteen aircraft operating that night.

> My last operation on 617 was a trip to Politz, which is near Stettin on the Russo-Polish border. We were going to bomb the big fuel storage depots. Now, you've got to remember it was the twenty-first of December and the weather was absolutely foul. It was pretty foggy, very cold. We were briefed, taken out to our aircraft, fired everything up, tested the engines ready to taxi out and the operation was cancelled or suspended. So we shut down the engines, got out of the aircraft [and] went all the way back to the flights again. I don't know what we did, we just wasted our time. And then some time later, maybe hours, it was back on. What the holdup was who knows? Poor old Joppy crashed his head on the rack inside the crew bus taking us out to the aircraft really hard. We got in the aircraft as normal and off we went. When we took off it was pitch dark and foggy, we just disappeared into the mist as it were, and off we went.
>
> I have to say the flight wasn't too bad. We weren't intercepted by fighters. There was the usual flak over the target. But I have to add here that our bomb-aimer, Lofty Hebbard, a New Zealander,

was in sick quarters, he'd got flu or a very heavy cold. Joppy was approached by Flight Lieutenant Arthur Walker, another bomb-aimer. He needed one more trip to complete forty-five operations, a double tour. He asked Joppy if he could become bomb-aimer. Well obviously Joppy was very pleased to have him. This lovely chap flew with us and did the bombing on the target successfully. We turned round and headed for home.

Operationally the Politz trip was successful. Despite the terrible weather the refinery was badly damaged and only three Lancasters out of a force of more than 200 were lost. The worst of it, however, was yet to come.

When we got back the fuel state wasn't really all that marvellous on our aircraft. I don't know why but it wasn't and everything was clamped down with thick fog. Woodhall Spa? There was no way we could get in there. So Joppy decided to head for Ludford Magna which had a FIDO installation. This was a much shorter airfield but at least it had got FIDO. We called up to try and get permission to land and so did about what sounded like a hundred others. The air was just jammed with people calling in. So, we were circling around, and this is where there is a point of discrepancy between my evidence and what the court of enquiry found. Without any warning at all there was a terrific bang. I looked out the port side and the wing just outside the port outer [engine] folded up. My gauges where going all over the place. The revs were up and down all over the place. Joppy yelled 'Full power! Full power!' I pushed everything through the gate. Nothing happened. Joppy called out, 'T Tear crashing! T Tear crashing!' And then he said, 'Ditching stations! Everybody to ditching stations!' Arthur Walker was just behind where I would normally stand and whether he heard us or not I don't know but he went forward into the bomb-aimer's compartment. Basil and I headed for our ditching station which was between the two spars, the main spar and the rear spar. Basil went first, I didn't see him again and I just flung myself over the front spar and the next minute we hit the ground with a terrific bang. Of course, the aircraft started burning as it would do. I seem to remember seeing flames over where the wireless op was and I tried to get up but I couldn't because somehow or other my parachute harness had got caught on something.

But you don't panic in those sorts of situations. Fortunately I thought, 'Christ, I've got to release myself'. So I twisted the buckle on my parachute, punched it and freed myself. And I got up and fell right down again. My leg was broken. So, now I'd got one leg and there was Basil standing up holding his head. I sort of woke him up, 'Come on Basil we've got to get out of here'. Part of your training tells you how to use the escape exits but it just shows you really how daft things happen. I went to my escape hatch which is in the roof and freed it, climbed out and fell over the side and crawled away from all this burning aircraft. Basil did the sensible thing, he went out through the back door, which I could have done easily. We subsequently found that the mid-upper gunner, we didn't have a mid-upper turret remember, still left over from *Tirpitz*, he was sitting on the 'second dickie', and he must have just got smashed in the initial impact and I don't know what happened to Cookie. I think he stayed in his place because he had bashed his head on his wireless set. Basil to his credit rescued Joppy from his seat. Joppy was very badly injured. Both his legs and his ankles were all tangled up in the rudder pedals. Basil lifted Joppy out and got him away from the aircraft. Poor old Arthur Walker, no sign of him. He must have been killed instantly because I expect the nose hit the ground first and when you think it was his last trip. His name is on the [Runnymede] memorial. That only leaves the rear gunner, Tommy Thompson. Now, Tommy Thompson had already done a tour when he joined us. As far as I know the turret broke off right across the field and hit something. The doors flew open and out shot Tommy. He broke his back but it was not so bad as you might think: they put him in a straitjacket and he was cured.

We lay out in this freezing field for about three and a half hours watching the aircraft burn. There was Joppy over one side, we were calling to each other. Cookie was wandering round in delirium which we subsequently found out was because the bang on the head had really brained him and he'd burnt his hand. Poor old Bob Yates, the mid-upper, was dead. Tommy was wandering around as well holding his back. And I was just lying there. I couldn't go very far on one leg. And we lay there absolutely freezing. Basil headed off across the fields and came across a farmhouse. Fortunately he had got his six-shooter with him as he woke up the farmer who was very, very good and took him down to a telephone box. I know it seems bizarre but we rang the operator and asked to be put through to the nearest RAF 'drome, which they did. Basil turfed out the ambulance and a team of squaddies and they brought stretchers and so forth and took us back to sick quarters. We were taken to the Louth County Infirmary, which was a civilian hospital, where we were X-rayed and given treatment. The next day the RAF 're-claimed' us in one of their boneshaking ambulances and took us to Rauceby. Rauceby was originally a lunatic asylum taken over the by the RAF and that was an eye opener. I was in the crash ward in Rauceby for a couple of days seeing sights that you wouldn't want to see again, including one poor chap in the next bed to me who'd lost both arms. That 'cheers' you up doesn't it? That's war but that was the end of my flying career. It upset me rather, I didn't want to know about RAF matters after that really, I just wanted to get the hell out of it. But I didn't fly anymore because by the time I'd come out of convalescence the war was over. They were talking about heading off to Japan with the Tiger Force but I wasn't selected for that, so I was sort of grounded.

Of Arthur Joplin's crew only Basil Fish went back onto operations during the war. Frank Tilley left the RAF and, at the time of writing, is retired and still takes a great interest in 617 Squadron activities.

Flight Sergeant Frank Tilley – Operations at 617 Squadron

- 27 August 1944 – Brest – Shipping. Merchant ships attacked to stop them being used to block Brest harbour. Successful operation.
- 23 September 1944 – Dortmund-Ems Canal – Canal banks. Successful attack as canal banks were breached and water drained from a long canal section. (Undertaken as part of Drew Wyness's crew.)
- 3 October 1944 – Westkapelle – Sea wall. Bombers brought their bombs back as an earlier raid had already breached the wall.
- 7 October 1944 – Kembs – Rhine barrage. Lock gates attacked successfully.
- 29 October 1944 – Tromso – *Tirpitz*. Target had moved closer to the UK so a direct attack was planned. Last-minute change in wind direction meant heavy cloud covered target. Tallboys dropped but no hits recorded.

- 12 November 1944 – Tromso – *Tirpitz*. Very successful attack as *Tirpitz* suffered at least two direct hits and capsized.
- 8 December 1944 – Urft Dam – Most crews did not drop their Tallboys due to very heavy cloud. Those who did saw no results and no hits were recorded.
- 11 December 1944 – Urft Dam – Still adverse weather over the target but some crews did bomb. Hits were recorded but no breach in the dam was made.
- 15 December 1944 – Ijmuiden – E-boat pens. Smokescreen hindered the bombing. Hits were seen on the pens but no results recorded.
- 21 December 1944 – Politz – Synthetic oil refinery. Heavy damage caused to refinery buildings and chimneys collapsed. Aircraft crashed on return when diverted due to fog.

Frank Tilley was posted from 617 Squadron as a war casualty on 22 December 1944.

Chapter 7

Flight Lieutenant Lawrence 'Benny' Goodman

I certainly wanted to fly. I did have a choice, fortunately, because I might have gone to the Army. But I volunteered well ahead of conscription although they didn't call me up for a long time.

Lawrence 'Benny' Goodman volunteered for the Royal Air Force towards the end of 1939 but it was a further year before he was actually called up for service.

I just wanted to get into the Air Force and I couldn't understand the delay. Obviously about a million other chaps were volunteering I think, and it was a very small Air Force before the war and they just couldn't cope with the number of people they were trying to induct.

I went and did my EFTS [Elementary Flying Training School] at Peterborough and, unfortunately, got selected. I still think it was a mistake as they were choosing people to be instructors after fifty hours of flying. I mean, I had very little experience. That was my total time and I and one or two others were selected to go on an instructors' course which we hated, all of us. But we were sent to Woodley in Reading to do the course. Suddenly, and you must appreciate there was a war on and all sorts of things happened, we were all then put on a boat to Canada and we did an SFTS, that's the Service Flying Training School on Ansons.

We finally got our wings and I became an instructor again, but this time with the Fleet Air Arm at Kingston, Ontario. It was enormous fun because I knew nothing about dive bombing or deck landings or deck take offs. We had to learn that before we could teach the acting leading naval airmen.

No. 31 Service Flying Training School in Ontario, Canada was an RCAF-administered centre but the majority of the students were training for the Fleet Air Arm. It must have seemed strange for an airman, trained in the ways of the RAF, to be instructing Naval trainees.

> I think you must look at this in the context of a huge war. It would be unique and unusual now but I wasn't the only one. I think there were altogether six of us. Three of us went to Kingston to the Fleet Air Arm training school. It was headed by a Lieutenant Commander. He was in charge but they were mostly RAF instructors with some Fleet Air Arm instructors who'd already been through the mill in the Fleet Air Arm. One chap was the last one to take off from the *Eagle*, which was sunk in the Mediterranean and he landed at Gibraltar. He took the very last Spitfire or Seafire and he couldn't get the wheels down and of course he made a belly landing. He was court martialled by the Navy which was typical of naval discipline at the time I think.

The future Naval airmen were trained on a few Fairey Battles which had been shipped out from the UK but the mainstay for the training was the North American T-6, one of the most popular training aircraft of the Second World war.

> We called them Harvards and I believe they are still in use – the T6 and the T6As – very good machines. They had an awful reputation for ground looping which I never understood because I never met anybody or saw anybody doing one. I had to learn first of all to fly it reasonably well at the time and then to do it from the back seat which was a little bit more difficult. But you, you just had to do what we were told, I mean, there was certainly enough care but you were only one step ahead of the student. You went up with an already qualified chap and he showed you what to do and then you took a student up and you showed him what to do. Obviously after two or three months you got pretty good at it but we did things like deck take-offs and jinking after take-off, dive-bombing, which was absolute fun in the lake right off almost at the end of the runway. Teaching when you're twenty or twenty-one and being told you can do this, it's paradise isn't it, being paid for it as well.

You didn't forget that there was a war on but certainly you wondered what you were doing there. I was then a pilot officer and I managed to buy a car for myself in Canada. I had digs in a house in the local town and it was extraordinary. But I and the three or four others knew that being an instructor and never having been on operations was looked down upon by everybody in the Air Force and we were all very keen to get back to the UK and take part in something. In fact, we jointly pestered the life out of the Wing Commander, Flying and he finally got us all a posting back to the UK. But it was a thoroughly enjoyable time flying these things. Aerobatics, dive-bombing, jinking after take-off – everything you'd normally get into awful trouble for in the RAF.

When we got back to England everything was in short supply. For a start there were blackouts and we all had to go on a course before we did anything else to get us used to flying in the UK, particularly after dark, because the whole country was blacked out. And so you had to learn how to navigate by nothing really.

Following a spell in hospital due to illness, Goodman was off flying duties for some time. Once he had recovered he resumed his training to become a front line bomber pilot.

By the time I was on my way to OTU I'd picked up another chap who'd been taken off front-line duties because he'd been in hospital. He was an observer and a bomb-aimer and we went to-gether to the OTU to pick up a crew. We stuck together through-out the whole of the war. In fact the crew we picked up at OTU, we stayed with.

You went into a huge room I'm not sure it was a hangar but a huge room and you looked at somebody and you thought, 'Mm he looks as if he might be a good chap' and if somebody else didn't grab him first you did. But somehow we all seemed to end up with the crews that we really liked afterwards and we trusted. Clearly on operations your life is in everybody else's hands and their lives are in your hands so it was an enormous amount of crew co-operation and loyalty.

To begin with nobody said 'you will fly with him and you come over here'. You did have the opportunity to talk to all the chaps first and I suppose it was a natural process really. A little bit haphazard, no doubt, but you thought to yourself: 'Well yes, I'll fly with him' or 'No wouldn't like to be with him, not by any means'. It worked out that way. You weren't given just ten minutes; you were given time to chat to people because after all you had to stay together, unless something happened, for some time.

We trusted each other implicitly, we had to. If you didn't trust somebody on your crew you shouldn't have been flying with them.

Complete with his crew Benny Goodman went on to his first four-engined bomber to get a real idea of the type of aircraft he would be flying on combat operations. No. 1660 Heavy Conversion Unit at Swinderby near Lincoln should have been using Lancasters but a shortage meant that Short Stirlings were used instead. The Short Stirling had been the first of the four-engined bombers to come into service with the RAF. Stirlings flew their first operation in February 1941, a raid on Rotterdam by, amongst others, three Stirlings of 7 Squadron. At that time the Stirling was the best bomber in service with the RAF but as the other 'heavies', the Lancaster and Halifax, developed, the Air Ministry's interest in the Stirling waned. Attacks by the Luftwaffe on Short's factories both in Rochester, in 1940, and later in Belfast, in 1941, had delayed production and proposals for improved versions were ignored. Thus Shorts never managed to fix the main problem which was a lack of engine power. This caused the aircraft to fly lower and slower than the other heavy bombers. Its bomb bay, while able to carry a heavy load, was not able to carry large bombs because of its sectioned design. Any target over 600 miles away meant that the Stirling could only carry a bomb load equivalent to that of a Wellington or even a Mosquito. By 1943 the aircraft was phased out from front-line bombing operations and relegated to glider-towing, minelaying and, increasingly, training of future heavy bomber crews.

When I first saw it and looked up into the cockpit I thought it was about twenty-seven feet off the ground. I thought that looks a bit of challenge. But it was the same for everybody.

It was like a ship inside and you had huge wheels for fuel tanks. You couldn't do it yourself. The flight engineer had to go back to the middle of the aircraft and turn these wheels around. But then it was built by Shorts of Belfast who usually built flying boats.

Once inside you got over the flight deck which was really, really capacious, you looked around and thought it more like the bridge of a ship. But once you were there and everybody was in place you were flying an aeroplane. It was more difficult on the ground actually for taxiing than it was in the air. Once in the air it was fine. It was a good aeroplane.

Our last trip was a sort of sortie. We did it with an instructor in the right-hand seat as a sort of shepherd pilot. It was to the Dutch coast or one of the Dutch islands which was a sort of operation because after all even on 617 we operated to the Dutch islands. But it was a night trip and it was just like another cross-country really. We saw nothing and heard nothing, I'm sure it was designed for that effect.

From Swinderby we were sent to an LFS, the Lancaster Finishing School, which was at Syerston near Nottingham. And we did the course, it was only ten or eleven hours on Lancasters and then you were considered fit to fly on operations. It looked good and it certainly flew well. It really was a very good machine and before the war was over it proved itself with the RAF. The boffins did anything they wanted with it and it still did exactly what you wanted as a pilot.

At the end of the course I was sent for by the flight commander, and I have to say I thought, and my crew thought, 'what the hell have I done wrong now?' I went into the flight commander's office and I thought even more that I'd done something wrong because there were three or four officers there and I thought this is really serious. The first question I was asked was, 'how would you like to join 617 Squadron?' I couldn't really believe my ears but they actually had asked me that and I mean, who wouldn't have jumped at the chance?

I think in all fairness it was generally always regarded and probably still is [as an elite unit]. I really couldn't believe it when I was offered it.

We would go as a crew. The whole crew had obviously been assessed. But I suppose the pilot was the captain and the captain's efficiency had to be first. But I don't know how they assessed us. They, of course, thought I was joking and that I had been in trouble but I finally convinced them we were selected and they were overjoyed like I was about it.

Until 1944 617 Squadron had been crewed by volunteers and selected experienced crews. At this point, August 1944, crews were being sent direct from Lancaster Finishing School for the first time.

> My first meeting was with Wing Commander Tait, he was a superb squadron commander. I felt really so awkward and out of place. There I was with these chaps; everybody knew who they were and I still couldn't believe that we were joining the squadron.
>
> Absolutely nobody was overbearing. It was a special duty squadron and we knew it but other than that we were ordinary chaps. We were very fortunate in having the SABS bomb-sight, for example, and providing you flew that properly then you knew you would do better than the average. But there was absolutely no sense of overbearing or better than the next chap. Absolutely not. In any case, it took me some time before I felt easy about being on the squadron. It took all of us time, I think.
>
> We could have been just another experienced crew, they were wonderful. Of course we had to go through more training with the squadron and we had to do more bombing practices. We had to be within a certain limit and then we were declared operational and then even after that I, as the captain, had to go as a second pilot to a very experienced and wonderful chap called Bob Knights who was very well-known pilot, an exceptional pilot. Even on that one trip I learnt a lot from him. After that we were declared operational. And that was it.

Benny Goodman went as second pilot on an operation with Bob Knights just two days after his posting to the Squadron. That operation was a daylight raid to la Pallice on the west coast of France, north of Bordeaux. The target was hardened U-boat pens and the raid was successful with a number of Tallboys scoring direct hits.

> We didn't often carry 1,000-pounders; we normally carried a Tallboy, that was 12,000 pounds and later some of us were lucky enough to carry the Grand Slam which was 22,000 pounds – that's 10 tons of bomb, and the Lancaster certainly wasn't designed for that. I think the bomb bay was modified slightly and I think we had the Lincoln undercarriage, if I remember correctly. And it just did the job. It was wonderful. A superb aeroplane.

We were all of us by then experienced pilots on the Lancaster and I can't remember any difficulty. One had to obviously fly it properly off the ground but it was fine. A little longer take off run as I recall but it did everything you asked it to do. It was a thoroughbred.

Despite the success of 617 Squadron and its relatively small number of losses, the training and preparation for operations was just as thorough as it would be for any other squadron in Bomber Command.

Briefing was on fairly normal lines. Obviously, you were told the target, the planning, the winds, the anti-aircraft fire you could expect, and any fighters that you might expect and so on. That was the general briefing and then the bomb-aimers went for their briefing, navigators went for theirs, the gunners and so on and you went usually went into briefing with your navigator. He did the plotting of courses and you watched him and you talked it over together. Then, you normally went back for a meal, a flying meal which was always the same. It was delicious. Remember, there was rationing in those days but we were always very well fed. And then you waited for the transport to take you out to the aircraft. I suppose waiting for either a flare to go up from air traffic control to say we can get in and start up, waiting there on the grass beside the aircraft, that was probably the most taxing time. It might be a very cold winter's night or a very bright summer's day but, once you got into the aeroplane, you had things to do, you settled down. You just thought of what you had to do and that was it, you just went ahead and did it.'

That quiet period before the start of an operation could be a difficult time but everyone dealt with it in their own way.

Everybody felt the tension but you spoke about what you might do when you got back next morning or what you might do that night when you got back. One or two of us might have spoken about the latest girlfriend or you had a date or you didn't have a date, that sort of thing. Anybody who says they'd never been frightened has never, as far as the RAF is concerned, been on ops, or they've never been facing opposition. That's all I can say, because when you're actually doing it you don't really have time to be frightened but it's afterwards or before.

One thing for the crews to get used to was the changing configuration of the aircraft, often different from one raid to the next.

> We mostly flew without the mid-upper turret, not always but mostly. For example, for the *Tirpitz* trip the whole of the inside of the fuselage was one massive, well two, fuel tanks actually. We weren't given the choice but given that the whole of the inside of the fuselage was two fuel tanks a spark would have been enough to blow the aircraft up.
>
> Nobody dwelt too much on enemy fighters because there could have been fighter opposition but fortunately they never got there in time.

These changes for the *Tirpitz* raids meant that the aircraft had a much higher fuel capacity and substantially increased range.

No. 617 Squadron's first attack on the German battleship *Tirpitz* had been on 15 September 1944. Having tested the maximum range of their aircraft, it was decided that it was too far to fly the mission direct from the UK. In company with aircraft from 9 Squadron they flew to Yagodnik in Russia before taking off again and making their attack. Although the ship was not sunk she still took one direct hit from a Tallboy. The German early warning system allowed the defences to lay an impenetrable smokescreen and the rest of the bombing was inaccurate. In October they tried again. After the September raid the Germans had decided to move *Tirpitz* out of Alten Fjord and into a shallower berth at Tromso. That was 200 miles nearer and just brought her within range of the UK mainland. On October 28 1944 aircraft from 617 and 9 Squadrons flew to Lossiemouth in Northern Scotland before refuelling and flying direct to Tromso on the 29th.

> I think we did know we would go again because the first trip was to Russia and it had been aborted. So we all knew it was bound to happen again.
>
> All the kudos must go to the navigators and the bomb-aimers, because all we did as pilots was take the aircraft off, fly what we told to fly by the navigator and on the run up, do exactly as the bomb-aimer said and so we were in their hands. We were, as they

all loved to call us, just the 'taxi driver'. Taking them someplace and coming back again.

It would have been beyond the Lancaster if they hadn't put the fuel tanks in the fuselage. But I think the whole trip was about thirteen and a quarter hours and I think that was pretty average. Everybody did it within that time and everybody had enough fuel to get back.

I didn't see it [*Tirpitz*] half as well as the bomb-aimer, of course. He had his sights for the run up which was some minutes long.

If I remember rightly they'd put up a smokescreen and we couldn't see the target very well. We had to see the target to bomb it accurately with the SABS bomb-sight and that was the reason that, although we got back, we hadn't done the damage that we hoped to have done.

I think it was probably the element of surprise as far as the fighters were concerned. They probably couldn't believe there was anybody until the raid started actually.

Really, it was tiring but we never seemed to notice it. The only time I did was after the *Tirpitz* trip, I needed a sleep. Thirteen and a quarter hours in one seat is quite a long time.

The attack was less successful than the September operation due to bad luck with the weather. Clouds rolled in thirty seconds before the first planned bomb drop and the target was obscured for most of the attack. Benny Goodman dropped his bomb but, as with most of the attacking aircraft, he failed to see either the bomb burst or what the results were. 617 Squadron were going to have to go back again.

The *Tirpitz* operations were some of the longest of the war for Benny Goodman and his crew.

It was a long time but you'd be surprised how occupied you were. Once you were over enemy territory, you couldn't just sit back. And on night trips particularly you didn't know if you were going to get jumped or not by a night-fighter. The Stettin raid, the oil refinery and plant, was quite a long way. It was about a six to six and a quarter hours trip all at night. It was, well, you're on the lookout as everybody is. You can't while away the time, you can't daydream. You had checks every now and again to reset the compass and the navigator wanted winds if he could get them.

These were things that you could do and did do. And you talked to the crew, I don't think you chatted, but you talked to the crew.

The need to stay alert and be aware of what was going on around you was a lesson crews ignored at their peril.

The weather in January 1945 was some of the worst on record. Heavy snow falls prevented flying for much of the month but a break meant that 617 flew their only operation, an attack on the U-boat pens at Bergen in Norway, on 12 January.

What I remember about Bergen was that it was a daylight operation. I can't remember exactly how many but we lost maybe four or five aircraft which is a lot to lose. We had Mustang escorts but the ack-ack opened up on us and our escort went down to shut them up. When that happened we were jumped by a squadron of Focke Wulf 190s which wasn't very nice indeed. And I think they just used us as a sort of 'Sally Ann'. It was not a very good day really. We never felt helpless, we knew what we'd got on our plates but we were just even more aware, if it's possible to be, watching out for these Focke Wulfs and waiting for an attack on each aircraft. You were lucky if you if you weren't attacked.

The squadron lost three aircraft to fighters that day and a fourth, that of Squadron Leader Tony Iveson, was badly damaged although he managed to get the aircraft home. Heavy damage was caused to the U-boat pens as at least three Tallboys penetrated the roof and demolished offices and workshops as well as damaging two U-boats.

On 14 March 1945 crews from 617 Squadron, including Benny Goodman's, were briefed to attack the Bielefeld viaduct which carried the vital rail link from the Ruhr Valley to Berlin and stood half way between Dortmund and Hanover. The squadron had been briefed initially for the operation twice in February and then on 9 March, which was abandoned due to low cloud over the target. The situation was similar on 13 March but this time two of the crews, those of 617's commanding officer, Johnny Fauquier, and Squadron Leader Jock Calder, were frustrated more than most as they were carrying the first Grand Slam ten-ton bombs and wanted to see them in operation against an important target. The operation finally went ahead the next day.

You were told, in the usual way; who was going; Tallboys, and who was carrying a Grand Slam. Any fighters; what the ack-ack was like, winds, that sort of thing. As a viaduct, of course, you had to get jolly close to it to destroy it.

The bomb-aimer was the one who said yes, he had, and of course we always took, whether we liked it or not, a photograph of our own bomb and flight of it over the target. It was automatically taken when the bomb-aimer pressed the button.' (In fact Benny Goodman's bomb had hit the railway itself.)

I can't remember how many times I went back, I think perhaps twice. We hoped we got it. Obviously our reputation depended. Of course it wasn't our fault always. If there was cloud cover you didn't drop the bomb. You brought it back.

One of the great things about the Tallboy and the Grand Slam was that if you got hit by flak it had such a great big thick shell on it that it took the flak and not you. So it was a protection and it was safe to land with whereas if you had a cookie on board – that was the 4,000-pounder – that was very dangerous to land with because it could easily detonate, any reason at all: a hard landing or it dropped or something, everything went up . With the Tallboy it was safe you could actually release it afterwards and let it drop on the ground as sometimes they had to – it happened once or twice when the aircraft was damaged. Of course it was disarmed but it was very good protection really.

The attack on 14 March proved the phenomenal capability of the Grand Slam bomb and the innovation of its designer, Barnes Wallis. It was the biggest bomb built during the whole war on either side. Earlier in the war it had been thought impractical as most believed that no aircraft would be strong enough to carry such a heavy bomb with such large dimensions. The Lancaster had proved that carrying a Tallboy was well within its capabilities, so this larger bomb was developed. It was immense at more than eight metres in length with a diameter of more than a metre. On release the bomb fell at supersonic speed and penetrated deep into the ground before exploding and creating an earthquake effect. This is exactly what happened to the Bielefeld viaduct when Jock Calder dropped his Grand Slam bringing down more than 250 metres of the viaduct with his single bomb.

On 19 March 1945 Goodman and his crew dropped their first ten-ton Grand Slam on another viaduct at Arnsberg east of the Ruhr Valley.

The target was destroyed with a section of more than twelve metres being demolished.

> The Lancaster was a wonderful workhorse. It was fine to fly with a Grand Slam but what I did notice on release was that we rose very rapidly several hundred feet in the air. My flight engineer said that he also heard a loud bang, but I never heard it, but he said he did. All I felt was this tremendous jump in the air.'

Perhaps Benny Goodman's worst moment came on his way home after an attack on U-boat pens at Hamburg on 9 April 1945.

> We had been doing a daylight on Hamburg, the port and we were coming back and my flight engineer who sat next to me in the jump seat as we called it – over Germany two pairs of eyes were obviously much better than one – he nudged me and sort of nodded his head. I looked down at the instruments and I could see nothing wrong so I went on flying. So he nudged me rather harder and moved his head more. I looked out of the starboard window and I was horrified to see the latest German fighter, an Me 262, in formation with us. I really thought: 'well he's having a look at us before he shoots us out of the sky and there's nothing we can do about it'. I don't know why he didn't except [that] he looked at us and I have to say there was no waving of hands and that sort of thing. We were absolutely horrified to see this thing there and he suddenly disappeared as quickly as he came. It seemed like two hours later but I think it was about thirty seconds or forty five seconds later and he disappeared. The only assumption we made afterwards was that he'd run out of ammunition and he either came to look at us out of curiosity, which was a bit dicey from his point of view, unless he came up from underneath, which I think he must have done, then we couldn't have shot at him anyhow, or his controller had said look at this Lancaster and tell us what you see or whatever else. Anyhow, he left us which was the important thing from our point of view, but that was extraordinary.
>
> If we had to get away we had the famous 5 Group corkscrew which we used to practice. It was really diving and climbing the Lancaster in a corkscrew fashion, diving one way then rolling

and still diving and then pulling up and rolling the other way and climbing on the way up and while we were still climbing going through the whole process again. You called out what you were doing so the rear gunner knew what to lay off on his gun-sight to get a bead on the enemy fighter. We were all young chaps and pretty fit and it becomes very much less demanding if you're trying to escape an enemy fighter I can tell you. You had to use a bit of muscle but nothing out of the ordinary. We, once or twice, had to do it in daylight. We never shot anybody down but more fortunately we weren't shot down.

The following month, on 25 April 1945, the squadron took part in an operation to attack Hitler's holiday retreat in the Bavarian Alps, Berchtesgaden.

Hitler's home, his 'Eagle's Nest'. We were a special duty squadron and that was a special duty I suppose. But I expected far more opposition than there was, being the place that it was, I thought there would be. But we bombed it and there was some opposition, but it wasn't as much as I thought there might be. This was right at the end of the war so possibly they weren't able to muster as much but I thought there would be even more because it was after all Hitler's 'Eagle's Nest' as he called it. The last thing I did was Berchtesgaden. That was the last trip, I didn't know it at the time but it was.

Flight Lieutenant Lawrence 'Benny' Goodman – Operations at 617 Squadron

- 18 August 1944 – la Pallice – U-boat pens. Successful operation. 'Second dickie' trip with Bob Knights' crew.
- 27 August 1944 – Brest – Shipping. Merchant ships attacked to stop them being used to block Brest harbour. Successful operation.
- 3 October 1944 – Westkapelle – Sea wall. Bombers brought their bombs back as an earlier raid had already breached the wall.
- 29 October 1944 – Tromso – *Tirpitz*. Target had moved closer to the UK so a direct attack was planned. Last-minute change in wind direction meant heavy cloud covered target. Tallboys dropped but no hits recorded.

- 8 December 1944 – Urft Dam – Most crews did not drop their Tallboys due to very heavy cloud. Those who did saw no results and no hits were recorded.
- 11 December 1944 – Urft Dam – Still adverse weather over the target but some crews did bomb. Hits were recorded but no breach in the dam was made.
- 15 December 1944 – Ijmuiden – E-boat pens. Smokescreen hindered the bombing. Hits were seen on the pens but no results recorded.
- 21 December 1944 – Politz – Synthetic oil refinery. Heavy damage caused to refinery buildings and chimneys collapsed.
- 29 December 1944 – Rotterdam E-boat pens. Successful operation with a number of hits recorded.
- 30 December 1944 – Ijmuiden – E-boat pens. Mission abandoned due to bad weather conditions over the target.
- 31 December 1944 – Oslo Fjord – Shipping. Illuminating and bombing shipping but no hits were registered.
- 12 January 1945 – Bergen – Shipping and U-boat pens. Successful operation in that many hits were registered on the pens and on shipping in Bergen harbour. However, two Lancasters were lost and a third was badly damaged.
- 3 February 1945 – Poortershaven – Midget submarine pens. Very successful operation with a number of hits being recorded.
- 8 February 1945 – Ijmuiden – E-boat pens. Highly successful operation as the remaining parts of the target were finally destroyed with large areas of the concrete roof falling and blocking the pens.
- 14 February 1945 – Bielefeld Viaduct – Mission abandoned due to heavy cloud over the target.
- 22 February 1945 – Bielefeld Viaduct – Much improved weather meant that the squadron could bomb the target finally. However, little damage was done which was rapidly repaired.
- 9 March 1945 – Bielefeld Viaduct – Mission abandoned due to bad weather over the target.
- 13 March 1945 – Bielefeld Viaduct – First time Grand Slam bombs were carried but heavy cloud over the target meant that both of them were brought back along with the Tallboys carried by the other aircraft.
- 14 March 1945 – Bielefeld Viaduct – Finally this series of attacks came to an end when the Grand Slam from 'Jock' Calder's

aircraft destroyed seven arches and rendered the viaduct completely unusable. One ten-ton bomb had managed what 3,500 tons of bombs had previously failed to do in numerous raids during the war.

- 19 March 1945 – Arnsberg Viaduct – Successful operation as six Grand Slams and thirteen Tallboys destroyed the viaduct.
- 21 March 1945 – Bremen – Arbergen railway bridge. Successful operation as target heavily damaged and put out of use.
- 22 March 1945 – Nienburg – Railway bridge. Successful operation as the bridge was destroyed.
- 23 March 1945 – Bremen – Railway bridge. Successful operation. Target destroyed.
- 27 March 1945 – Farge – U-boat pens. Very successful operation as newly finished twenty-three foot thick concrete roof was destroyed and thousands of tons of concrete made the pens totally unusable.
- 6 April 1945 – Ijmuiden – Shipping. Mission aborted due to heavy cloud over target.
- 7 April 1945 – Ijmuiden – Shipping. Improved weather meant that the operation went ahead with several hits being recorded.
- 9 April 1945 – Hamburg – U-boat pens. Successful operation. Several hits severely damaged the pens.
- 13 April 1945 – Schweinemunde – Shipping. Bad weather caused the operation to be aborted.
- 25 April 1945 – Berchtesgaden – The Eagle's Nest. Hitler's home in the Bavarian Alps attacked successfully with much damage being done to houses and barracks in the area. This was 617 Squadron's final operation of the war.

Benny Goodman was posted to 102 Squadron from 617 Squadron on 10 May 1945.

Chapter 8

Pilot Officer Murray Vagnolini (Valentine)

Perhaps Vagnolini was not the best surname for a man in Bomber Command during the war but Murray couldn't change his name to Valentine because there was already another Valentine in the squadron, so Vagnolini he would stay.

> My name was Vagnolini. My great-grandfather came to this country from Italy. I was known at the squadron, certainly on 617, as 'Musso'. Everybody knew me as 'Musso'. At the end of the war, when I was offered a short service commission, I decided to change it to Valentine as it was so much easier on the telephone.

Murray always had a connection to flying and the Air Force but it was his experience of the impact of war on his family that set him on a career path with the Royal Air Force.

> What made me go into the Air Force, particularly into Bomber Command, was the fact that I was evacuated to Orpington in Kent right in the middle of the Battle of Britain. Seeing my family sheltering under the table when we were being bombed nightly made me feel I wanted to do something about it. Hence I went into Bomber Command and I couldn't wait for my service to come through.
>
> I enlisted at seventeen but I was deferred until I was eighteen and a quarter. I stayed there [in Orpington] because I got a very good job in Orpington High Street. And then I eventually got a job as a despatch rider with the ARP. That was considered war work but they did phone me up a couple of times and say it could be reviewed as they particularly wanted aircrew at that time.
>
> We realised, as the war went on, that we were 7 miles from Biggin Hill and we'd actually been evacuated to the centre of the

Battle of Britain. Oh, it was fantastic! I thought it was great watching the Battle of Britain there. We had a Spitfire crash-land in the field just by my uncle's house. We all went over there and saw a chap who couldn't speak English but he wasn't German, he was a Pole, from a Polish squadron at Biggin Hill. I used to go up to Biggin Hill with the Air Training Corps quite often and help up there, wash the windows down from the blood from a pilot who had been wounded and, oh dear, a most interesting time there. But that was all rubbed out when the Blitz started of course. Orpington is up the Thames just where they, if they were attacked and in trouble, would often drop their bomb loads, let alone that they were bombing Bromley and places like that with the aircraft manufacturers round there. [After I joined up] I would come home on leave there. It was too far for me to go on leave to my wife in Scotland so I'd take short leaves there. I was glad sometimes to get back off leave; I was down the blasted shelter being bombed to hell in Orpington.

Murray Valentine was finally called up in 1942. He then started the long training required for aircrew that would see him finally become operational in 1944.

I eventually got my call up papers and reported to Royal Air Force Padgate, near Warrington, the biggest recruiting centre in the country. I know that because, eventually, eight or nine years later I went back there as station adjutant. And then I used to hand over to Group Captain Dark. I used to hand over to him 4,700 men on parade, 'Sir'. Quite a recruiting centre!

It was going away knowing that my aircrew training could be two years before I became operational. I wanted to make sure that I was selected to go as a pilot, as I had applied for. However, I was transferred to the radio or wireless section as it was called. So I went in as a wireless operator/air gunner.

The radio or wireless side of it was a considerably long ground course, four months to start with after my basic sixteen weeks at Blackpool. That, plus operational aircrew training, finally getting selected by a pilot to go in the crew and then the pilot having to convert from two and three engines to four engines and this all took time. Eventually it took me two years after I entered the service to become operational.

You were supposed to be very technically concerned because the initial ground course for radio or wireless operating was four months and it was extremely 'eight in the morning until five in the evening' training. When you passed the ground course you were selected as aircrew.

Eventually wireless operator/air gunners began to be handed over to be trained as straight air gunners. I did an emergency two-week course training as a gunner and then I was sent on a navigator's course to Scotland for sixteen weeks. So I was really a radio navigator. This was when radar was coming in.

During the early period of the war the standard wireless equipment in RAF bombers was the R1082 receiver and the T1083 transmitter. These were universally used in all bombers including the Fairey Battle, Vickers Wellington, Handley-Page Hampden and Armstrong Whitworth Whitley. It was, however, considered to be virtually obsolete by 1939.

The ten-eighty-twos and ten-eighty-threes which I originally started on were changed and we took over on eleven-fifty-five radios and eleven-fifty-four transmitters which had an eighty-foot aerial to let out and had something up to 2,000 miles range. And that's why I changed over almost in the middle of my training which extended it, I think.

The replacements for the obsolete early war wirelesses were masterminded by a design team at Marconi led by Christopher Cockerell, who was later knighted for his invention of the hovercraft. The R1155 receiver and T1154 transmitter became the standard communication equipment in Lancaster and Halifax bombers, as well as other RAF aircraft. They were easier to operate, provided a better performance and had a wider range of frequencies than anything that the RAF had used before, essential as countermeasures and jamming were increasingly used by Germany. Eventually more than 80,000 sets were manufactured.

It was all heavily fixed into the aircraft. And heavily tested and checked and signed to that effect by the ground technician when you got into the aircraft. He was then handing you over a perfectly serviced receiver and transmitter.

I think the radio navigator, particularly in Bomber Command, became more connected with the navigation because of the range we had. The navigator would, from time to time, ask for a fix or a radio direction which I could pass to him just to satisfy him in his own mind [about] his positioning and direction.

One of the things you could do navigationally was to get accurate QDMs which were magnetic headings to steer directly back to base. In the event of an emergency, if you were out over the North Sea miles from anywhere, you could get a fix. I got them on occasions when the navigator was completely lost, possibly through bad weather. It used three stations which got a bearing on you and where they crossed becomes a triangle. You could get one-to-three clarity. One was zero to five miles accurate; two I think was ten to fifteen miles and three clarity was probably twenty-five miles. You had forty-three stations listening out in your area. But, you were always there and in great demand as a radioman for air-sea rescue because you were the last one to give the position where you might come down. I think navigators felt that if they were using the radio they were letting themselves down rather than getting help but if you were going down in the drink you were getting a fix before you went down.

The radio equipment you took with you into the dinghy when you ditched, that was your responsibility. It was manually operated and you put your aerial up in a kite. It was then who's going to get you first. Whether you would be picked up by a German air-sea rescue or British air-sea rescue ... And sometimes it was a race to get there and they had a shoot up between them over who's going to pick you out of the drink.

The new receivers also had an eighty-foot-long aerial which had to be let out.

The training from the technicians always assumed we let it out but we didn't always because I could pick up the UK quite satisfactorily on the fixed aerial, apart possibly from when I went to Koenigsburg. Of course it had another use because when ditching allowing for the trail on it you had eighteen lead balls and the last one is a brass ball for some unknown reason when it was out on full trail eighty feet. When the pilot was ditching, if you put your transmitter on when the trailing aerial touched the water you told the pilot we were 50 feet allowing for the trail on it and it gave him some idea if he was ditching in the dark. That was it, that's the use of the trailing aerial in an emergency.

During training Murray had his one and only experience of what was called LMF. Lack of Moral Fibre was the RAF's way of describing many situations. It could be anything from refusing to fly on operations, becoming 'flak happy', as suffering from operational fatigue would be called, to not returning to base after leave.

A pal of mine went home and got engaged to his girlfriend and he went absent. He got engaged and his girlfriend wouldn't continue it unless he packed up flying. He was court-martialled for deserting because he went over the month, over thirty days. He was LMF, Lack of Moral Fibre. I don't know what happened to him after the court martial. So he didn't reach the squadron. Sad.

Murray's final training was at 14 OTU where he flew in Wellingtons. This unit specialised in training night-bomber crews.

I was at an Operational Training Unit, 14 OTU Market Harborough in Leicestershire, and it wasn't until the end of training that eventually I was approached by a pilot and asked if I had got a crew? I said, 'No I haven't been crewed.' I found out afterwards [that] he had been to the Signals Leader to find out what sort of chap and how careful or capable I was. He asked me would I like to join the crew. He was a Canadian Flying Officer, Nelson Hill, who took me into his crew and with five others we formed a successful crew and fortunately finished a successful tour of operations, thirty trips.

Nelson Hill was born in Innesfall, Alberta in 1922 before moving and spending much of his early life in Toronto. He enlisted on 29 December 1941 and trained in Canada before eventually being commissioned in February 1943 and coming to the UK.

We were a very close crew, very much so in my first tour. The fact that once we were almost on the target and we got a recall and were diverted due to the weather situation to some way away from our airfield, I think the crew realised the reliability and the essentialness of the radio operator.

Wireless operators had very rigid rules about using their radio on a trip.

As far as the radio operator was concerned it was radio silence throughout the trip until on return or in an emergency which I didn't have on many occasions. On our return to base you broke radio silence in the circuit to show you were home. Other than that it was a call from Bomber Command Headquarters every quarter of an hour. If you did get a message which was recalling you or diverting you it was all done in code of course. That's where your training as a radio operative came in.

Although it doesn't sound much, you had to get your every message down and it was entered on a log, regardless of enemy action during that time. There was a man who would confirm and have words with you over the fact that you hadn't neatly under-lined your log book, even if you had just been attacked by an enemy aircraft. That was discipline.

Nelson Hill and his crew seemed to have no problem getting to know each other and gelling as an operational team.

There was so much operational training. Twelve weeks at OTU and onto the advanced flying unit, another twelve weeks together. At that time I was a non-commissioned officer and half the crew were not on commission so we spent a lot of our social life together. I think that working with the amount of flying time we put in, together with operational flying time, we eventually formed a decent crew.

Two of us were English, the rest of the crew were Canadians. On my first tour they were Canadians and one American. His father was an Englishman from Liverpool and like a lot of [Americans] when the war broke out, he said he was a Liver-pudlian to get across and join the Canadian Air Force and get into the war.

We had no tension in our crew at all really but I fell out with one of my crew over a matter concerning our living conditions. We all lived in a Nissen hut as an NCO as I was then. But we made it up hurriedly because I always remember saying to him, 'Let's pack it up and stop arguing, let's finish the tour', which I wanted to do.

Along with the rest of the crew, Murray was posted to 61 Squadron at Skellingthorpe, three miles west of Lincoln. No. 61 Squadron had been a mainstay of Bomber Command's Main Force throughout the war and eventually would fly the second highest number of operations of all the Command's squadrons. Probably 61 Squadron's most famous pilot was Bill Reid who was awarded a VC in November 1943. Badly wounded during the operation Reid was hospitalised. Coincidentally Reid went on to 617 Squadron in January 1944 where he stayed for six months. In July 1944 his aircraft was hit by a bomb dropped from a Lancaster above, and with the aircraft rapidly falling apart he and the crew baled out. Reid spent the rest of the war as a PoW.

We knew 61 Squadron was a very well-known operational squadron and had been in the thick of it bombing for Bomber Command. But we were pleased to hear we were going there, mainly, I think, because we were near Lincoln city and not out in the wilds too much.

I've always remembered our Commanding Officer, a wing commander, an Australian. We went into the office with him and he said, 'Welcome to the Squadron. Just remember this. While you're here I expect you to have a short haircut, be well washed and shaved, clean underwear and well-pressed trousers.' Not shoes, because we wore flying boots, and he said, 'I tell you this because you and myself, we are all likely to be shot down at some time and that's how I expect you to be received by the enemy.' It was discipline and that's how he felt about it, particularly on the underwear. He didn't want us going over there with dirty underwear to prison camps. Astonishing man.

During the years when the squadron operated Lancasters, between 1942 and 1945, 116 aircraft were lost over Europe. One of the biggest problems aircrew always had during their time on operations was dealing with the loss of other crewmen.

We had come back and one of the crews who was sharing our room, six of them, didn't come back and, of course. the [RAF] police used to clear the room of everything. If the crew was missing, all their belongings were sealed off and sent back to the next of kin and that was it. An empty hut till the next crew was posted. The hut was soon filled up. I think you took it for granted. You just went along with that sort of life and the chaps were there in the hut one moment and new people were in the next. One always hoped, there's always the hope, that they'd been shot down and made prisoners of war. We'd come back off leave and suddenly you'd hear that old so and so had gone. Perhaps three aircraft; I suppose it's not a lot of aircraft but that's twenty-one men from the officers' mess. Then you just heard old so and so had gone and then eventually we would hear they were prisoners of war which is rather nicer to hear.'

Otherwise, like all crewmen, Murray tried to live a normal squadron life.

We were very lucky, we were near Lincoln city and we used to go out. It was just 4 miles which we used to walk every evening as opposed to some of the satellites which were 15 miles from the local pub. We would see normal life and meet one or two people that I trained with because Lincoln was full of people. There were Waddington, Scampton and two or three satellites round there and Skellingthorpe, so I would go out with members of other crews, not necessarily spending all our time together. Life didn't seem so bad really; perhaps I was a bit blasé about it all. But I looked forward eventually to when the time came and you got back in the evenings and there was an operational notice on the board. You all got together and talked about it, wondering where we were going.

Murray and the crew arrived at 61 Squadron in June 1944, a very busy time. Just a few weeks earlier the invasion had taken place in Normandy and Bomber Command had spent its spring and early summer supporting the invasion by 'softening up' the enemy and attacking tactical targets such as railway yards, communications centres and ammunition dumps. Now the bombers directly supported the Allied forces on the ground. The crew finally went on their first operation on 18 July 1944, a daylight attack on two German divisions standing in the path of the Allied attack east of Caen, Operation GOODWOOD.

My first operation was quite memorable because it was a daylight raid and it was on Caen. There were German organisations held up inside one of the fortified villages and unfortunately we had to bomb it to hell with about sixty Lancasters. We saw a lot of action. Mainly you were watching your own aircraft with bomb bays open above you, worrying whether you were going to be struck by your own aircraft. We learned afterwards that the ones we had to be concerned about were the aircraft with bomb doors open behind us because the aircraft would shoot its bomb load forward at high speed and so we made sure, where possible, that we had no one above us. But that was my first trip: Caen, daylight, very short, about four hours operational.

In fact July 1944 was a very busy month for a new crew to be finding their way on operations. Between that first trip on 18 July and the end of the month Murray flew a further six operations, mostly against other tactical targets in France such as railway yards and flying-bomb sites. On 23 July, however, Bomber Command sent more than 600 air-craft, including Murray's Lancaster, to attack Kiel, their first large raid on a German city since before the Normandy invasion. Four days later they went to Stuttgart.

After those first trips I was doing several trips of six, seven, eight hours and my longest one which was to Königsburg, that was ten hours twenty-five minutes. And after that I did eight trips of seven or eight hours down into the Ruhr which was heavy firing all the time from the ground. Not so much night-fighters because they didn't take part where a lot of ground fire came up because they could be damaged themselves. But, during our tour, we did our fair share of long trips down into Germany.

Well, believe it or not, it seems very difficult to remember them now. I know we were badly shot up one evening when we went down into the Ruhr – a German target, Darmstadt or something like that. We had several cannon shells along the side over my head. We'd never had our gunners or anybody in the crew injured, as it happened, but we were badly shot up. We lost two engines but we managed to get back to Skellingthorpe. Königs-burg, of course, is very prominent as it was a very long arduous trip.

Perhaps Murray's most dangerous trip while on 61 Squadron came on the night of 11 November 1944 when they flew an operation to bomb an oil refinery at Harburg, south of Hamburg. Attacked by a Ju88 night-fighter the Lancaster was hit several times and badly damaged. Successfully completing their bombing run Nelson Hill was turning for home when they were hit again, this time by flak. Despite his stricken aircraft, Hill managed to get his crew safely back to Skellingthorpe. This operation was noted in particular when Hill was awarded his DFC early in 1945.

The daylight trips during the summer of 1944, mainly in support of ground operations in Normandy, gave the crews a chance to see much more than they were used to with their history of night operations.

I saw several unfortunate incidents where a stick of bombs from one of our aircraft hit another of our aircraft which peeled over and hit another one and there were just bodies tumbling through the sky which is very sad. Nowadays it's called 'friendly fire' and we had a lot of that on daylight raids.

As soon as you were not on the on the radio you took your post in the astrodome above you and kept your eyes open with the rest of the crew looking for fighters or keeping a watch, keeping a watch all the time. Then you went back to your radio and did your work.

All you saw was a complete sea of aircraft, that's all I can say. You would be watching particularly as you were on the run up to the bombing run. Aircraft would open their bomb doors and you might say to your pilot, 'Watch it skipper, there's one right above us, just behind', but he didn't really need to be told because his engineer would be pointing this out, sat beside him.

At night it was a different story.

You're looking into the darkness. There were several times when we were attacked and hit by night-fighters. I was actually on the radio and I never actually took part in sighting a night fighter. But it was always that feeling you're doing something. As soon as you finished receiving transmissions you would step up into the astrodome. It was only just to the side of the radio anyway. And then you'd look down the fuselage, you'd see your mid-upper turret, he'd be twirling round looking out and, of course, behind him would be our rear gunner. We were the three looking out for possible attacks from nightfighters.

We did have flying suits on but, because I was in the position where I controlled the heat for the aircraft and it was very warm, I often found myself with my battledress and my parachute harness off, in my shirt sleeves. One looks back and thinks what a fool you were.

The main thing you were concerned with was the sea you were travelling over and you were over enemy territory, so if you were shot down, which happened suddenly from flak or an aircraft, you should be geared up to bale out and one was never really prepared for that, looking back on it.

The gunners had their electric suits on, that's the mid-upper and the rear gunner, so I controlled the heat for myself, the navigator, engineer, pilot and bomb-aimer, up in the front. Quite often the pilot would flash me on the radio to say, 'Can you turn the heat down Murray?' or 'Would you turn the heat up?', which made it more uncomfortable for me, so one had to sort of come to an agreement.

You were so busy as far as I was concerned, as the radio man, in the job you were doing the fact of being shot down or shot up didn't come to you until it happened. You went into the aircraft, your job was there and you had a lot of work to do, as did the gunners. Their job was to look out and see we weren't attacked and the navigator was in his 'office' and had so much to do. We were all concerned that we were going to get there, get to the target so the bomb-aimer was happy, and then get home as quick as hell and land safely. We were only too happy having had our aircrew breakfast and got back to the mess to see there wasn't another operation up for the next night or the same day, which quite often happened I'm afraid.

Murray's final operation with his crew on 61 Squadron was to attack the U-boat pens at Trondheim on the night of 22 November 1944. Murray doesn't remember being tired or not ready to go on ops but does remember being relieved to have survived the tour. What he never expected was to go on a second tour almost immediately.

I was very pleased when it came up that we were finished. My pilot, we called him 'Uncle' because he was twenty-four, was engaged to a young lady in Canada for three years and he had a 'Dear John', as it was called in those days. It was a note telling him that she had married their GP, whom they both knew very well. That's when he decided that he would apply to go to 617 Squadron. My pilot came back and said he had been accepted and would I go with him and he said, 'Oh, you don't have to do anything if you'll come with me I can arrange it.' So myself and Les, the engineer, decided to go with him. In those days it was far better than being selected to go and do training lectures. I was very proud to go with him, and I was commissioned at that time, a different life again.

I was just entering the Officers' Mess and seeing more of my pilot and all the others. I remember I was told when I was going into the Officers' Mess to just 'keep quiet and watch and listen for six months. You'll learn a lot.'

We had 617 with us leading some of the daylight raids before I joined 617. So they seemed not to be specialising as much as I think they did when we had the larger bombs when I joined them later. So, you know I always assumed 617 was a normal squadron. It wasn't until we joined them I realised it was a special duty squadron.

Murray was posted to 617 Squadron at Woodhall Spa on 4 January 1945.

We found that we'd got weeks training with the special bomb-sight that 617 used, plus they had no mid-upper gunners, so there was only one gunner on the aircraft, so it was a different life when we met our new bomb-aimer and navigator. The gunnery leader was our gunner and we did nearly five weeks' training before they said that we were suitable to fly and eventually drop the 12,000-pounder and then the ten-tonner. I must say I got fed up with the training programme all the time. The Signals Leader was a very strict man on keeping tidy logs and Nelson was having a lot to learn with dropping the bigger bomb with what was a different aircraft really.

Our training was mainly in the use of the SABS, the Stabilised Automatic Bomb-Sight, which was what the squadron used. Apparently, the pilot and bomb-aimer relationship had to be very close for the use of it and we were all getting a bit fed up with how many training flights we had to do. Every day we went out [during] that five weeks' training period because the weather was good. We went down to the local Wainfleet bombing range and practised for the use of the bigger bombs. We had to have a lot of training and the bombs couldn't be wasted. Eventually we settled down and waited.

The crew's first operation at 617 Squadron was on 22 February 1945. A daylight trip, they flew to attack the Bielefeld viaduct in Northern Germany. In fact their first four operations at 617 would be to that same target.

As well as the viaduct the city of Bielefeld was also an essential target. As an industrial centre of its own it produced many types of guns and grenades as well as tank tracks and gun turrets. The railway that went through the area and used the viaduct, however, was the busiest in Germany with more than 300 trains using the line each day as they took materials backwards and forwards between Berlin and the Ruhr valley. One of the most vulnerable stretches was the 400-metre-long viaduct which was built to carry the railway across the river Werre. More than 3,000 tons of bombs had been dropped before 617 were tasked with destroying the viaduct. It was damaged in the attack on 22 February but rapidly repaired. Two further operations were planned for 9 and 13 March, and both were aborted. In both cases Murray's aircraft brought the Tallboy bomb back to base. It was not until 14 March that the viaduct was finally destroyed when Jock Calder dropped the first 22,000lb Grand Slam bomb.

As with the Upkeep bouncing bomb, the Tallboy and Grand Slam bombs had been invented by Barnes Wallis.

Everything really revolved around the Dams raid. I was brought forward as the youngest member of the crew to meet Barnes Wallis. He came and visited the squadron when we were dropping the Tallboy and getting ready to drop the ten-tonner. So it was a highly specialised squadron and I realised we were doing something very special.

He also designed the alterations to the Lancaster for the ten-tonner which would be held externally on the aircraft and formed part of the fuselage. The two arms that clasped the bomb were released and then it was my secondary duty, as the wireless operator, to climb over the main spar at the back and wind these two arms in because they were flying about in the air. This was something they didn't tell us, but when an aircraft dropped a bomb that size it leaps about 200 to 300 feet into the air and I suddenly found myself no longer on the ground holding these, winding in, but I was up on the ceiling of the aircraft.

There was also the experience of carrying my mobile ten-minute oxygen canister at the same time. You were plugged in and you could hear the bomb-aimer saying you were on the run, and when he said that we were on the run up, that was my [cue] to go back. The pilots were very keen on getting a photograph. My pilot was so keen on occasions, particularly in Main Force on my first tour, that he would go around again to make sure he got a decent photograph which isn't the sort of thing, looking back on it now, that one was very happy about.

After the Bielefeld viaduct the squadron was tasked with systematically destroying all the bridges that could carry material from the Ruhr valley to the front line. On 21 and 22 March 1945 Nelson Hill and his crew flew two successful operations to attack bridges near Bremen in Northern Germany. The Arbergen bridge and the Nienburg bridge were both destroyed under the weight of Grand Slams and Tallboys. Four days later Murray flew on his final operation of the war, to attack the massive concrete roof sheltering the U-boat pens at Farge on the river Weser, again in Bremen. The pens were hit by two Grand Slams which penetrated the roof to a depth of six metres. They were followed by a number of near misses from Tallboys, which undermined the whole structure. The pens were never used.

After the war Murray returned to Farge with Wing Commander Jock Calder to survey the scene on the ground.

I've a photo of me standing at one of these holes, that enormous crater. We went through about thirty or forty feet of concrete. But down below we could see there were about eight submarines all spun around when this bomb went down. So it did a jolly good job of attacking submarine pens.

Murray didn't take part in 617 Squadron's final operation but stayed on until the end of May 1945.

When the war ended I was spending a lot of time at the Woodhall Spa Hotel and just wondering what was going to happen with us all. They split us up, mainly because we'd done two tours. Everyone was thinking about the Far East. We heard that Cheshire had gone out there and was preparing for 617 to arrive. Of course, we didn't know about the large bomb that the Americans had, so everything reversed considerably when that came to light. Cheshire went on that raid with the Americans as an observer.

I certainly had it in view that I was going to go to the Far East if Nelson was going to go. Tiger Force was being formed and we were going to use the bigger bombs out there against the Japanese. And suddenly we found out we wouldn't be going. So we settled ourselves to thinking, 'Well the war's over now and how long will it be before I'm demobilised?' There was great talk then, of course, of people staying in and being given a career in the Air force.

I was offered a four-year extended service commission with a view to a permanent commission. I asked to go on flying duties and I was sent to 44 Squadron as Assistant Signals Leader at Wyton which I knew. They were on Lincolns when I arrived.

After a short time at 44 Squadron Murray decided to leave the service and took a job as a London welfare officer, going to court and enjoying the chance to lead a normal life and going home every evening. However, he soon missed the service and rejoined the RAF, staying until 1963 before retiring with the rank of flight lieutenant.

At the time of writing Murray and his wife still run a club on the south coast of England.

Pilot Officer Murray Vagnolini (Valentine) – Operations at 617 Squadron

- 22 February 1945 – Bielefeld – Viaduct. Much improved weather meant that the squadron could bomb the target finally. However, little damage was done and it was rapidly repaired.
- 9 March 1945 – Bielefeld – Viaduct. Mission abandoned due to bad weather over the target.
- 13 March 1945 – Bielefeld – Viaduct. First time Grand Slam bombs were carried but heavy cloud over the target meant that both of them were brought back along with the Tallboys carried by the other aircraft.

- 14 March 1945 – Bielefeld – Viaduct. Finally this series of attacks came to an end when the Grand Slam from 'Jock' Calder's aircraft destroyed seven arches and rendered the viaduct completely unusable. One ten-ton bomb had managed what 3,500 tons of bombs had previously failed to do in numerous raids during the war.
- 19 March 1945 – Arnsberg – Viaduct. Successful operation as six Grand Slam and thirteen Tallboys destroyed the viaduct.
- 21 March 1945 – Bremen – Arbergen railway bridge. Successful operation as target heavily damaged and put out of use.
- 22 March 1945 – Nienburg – Railway bridge. Successful operation as the bridge was destroyed.
- 23 March 1945 – Bremen – Railway bridge. Successful operation. Target destroyed.
- 27 March 1945 – Farge – U-boat pens. Very successful operation as newly finished twenty-three-foot-thick concrete roof was destroyed and thousands of tons of concrete made the pens totally unusable.

Murray Vagnolini was posted to 15 Squadron from 617 Squadron on 29 May 1945.

Chapter 9

Pilot Officer John Langston

Like many wartime aircrew John Langston was inspired as a small boy by aviation pioneer Sir Alan Cobham and his flying circuses. During the early 1930s Cobham would tour the country putting on barn-storming displays as well as taking members of the public up for their first flight.

> We were picnicking in South Devon with the family and they had a great big sign up saying flights for seven and sixpence [37.5p]. I had just had a birthday and I had seven and six and I said to my mother, 'I'm going to have a flight.' She said, 'Oh no, you're not,' so we had an argument and my mother gave in. So I had a flight with Pauline Gower who was a woman pilot who became head of the Air Transport Auxiliary. We took off and we flew around in this Spartan aeroplane. I had my eldest sister with me and to keep me down they strapped me in and all I could see was a piece of green plywood in front of me vibrating away, and every time I tried to undo the straps to look out my sister banged me back down into the cockpit. And so we flew around the circuit and it was only when we finally banked to come into land that I had my first glimpse of the ground. And so I had my flight and that was the start of it. That was 1933.

In fact Pauline Gower had a very distinguished aviation career, first running an air taxi and joyriding business in Kent, then flying with Sir Alan Cobham before becoming the head of the Women's Branch of the ATA. She was responsible for all the recruiting, training and running of the service which delivered thousands of aircraft from manufac-turer to squadron during the war. Sadly her life was cut short when she died in 1947, at the age of just thirty-seven, while giving birth to twins.

This early flying experience had John Langston hooked and he took every opportunity to get more flying hours.

At school I was in the Air Training Corps at the start of the war and I used to go to Exeter airport which was used by some of the Battle of Britain fighter squadrons. 601, I remember was down there and we used to be allowed to clean the windshields and things at the weekends. So, about once a month, we'd go out to the airport and we even used to do quite extraordinary things like prepare parachutes for packing and things that kept us busy. At school my best friend got one of these RAF wartime quick scholarships for university into the service and so I naturally followed and, in 1941, I applied for an RAF wartime university scholarship and was fortunate enough to go to Oxford. We used to go down to Abingdon from the university air squadron at the weekends and fly Tiger Moths and so that meant that I didn't have to do ITW [Initial Training Wing] when I joined the service in October 1942. And so from there it was straight to grading school and then straight across the Atlantic to Canada.

A lot of the immediate pre-war recruiting was done directly through the university air squadrons. In the years following the First World War Hugh Trenchard set out to ensure the long-term survival of the RAF as an independent service. He recognised that a core of intelligent people was needed for the Royal Air Force, so what could be a better way to enthuse undergraduates than by giving them the opportunity of learning to fly while studying at their universities. John Langston's squadron at Oxford had been one of the first two formed in 1925 and was responsible for many famous names learning to fly, including Leonard Cheshire.

We were just doing a couple of hours in Tiger Moths every other weekend at Abingdon. But it was a wonderful way in. We were taught to strip machine guns, we were taught the rudiments of navigation, we were taught the rudiments of airmanship and things like that and we did drill and all the things that one did at an ITW. But we were excused all that so, when we were recruited, we got into the service, we were kitted out and we went straight into the training pipeline. We went from Oxford and my next stop was Lord's cricket ground along with all the other air crew that were recruited. I can remember in the Long Room at Lords we all gave our last three numbers and raised our hands and got our first pay grade. And in the room under the Long Room we were all kitted out with our first uniforms, so that was the way in. I was young, I was dead keen as mustard on the service, on flying and all the chaps I was with were equally keen. We were aiming to get our training, get our wings and to fly and to be part of the service.

I went up to Perth in Scotland and did the grading course up there. I was selected to be a pilot and I did my first solos and things like that. Then it was a question of waiting to go to Canada for training.

John remembers his trip across the Atlantic very well.

Going out we went out on the *Queen Elizabeth* and we were sixteen or seventeen of us in bunks in the first-class compartments, but I mean it was a wartime fitted trooper really. We went into New York and I can remember passing the Statue of Liberty and as we docked at the Cunard pier, there was a ship lying on its side immediately beside us. It was the French ship the *Normandie* which had been sunk in the dock.

The SS *Normandie* was a French ocean liner which plied the Atlantic route from le Havre to New York many times during the late 1930s. At the outbreak of war *Normandie* was docked in New York and she was interned by US authorities. When France fell the following year she was seized and eventually taken over by the US Navy who changed her name to the USS *Lafayette* and planned to convert her to a troopship. In February 1942, during conversion, fire broke out and was soon out of control. Thousands of tons of water poured onto the fire caused the ship to develop a dangerous list. Early the following morning she capsized. Although attempts were made to salvage her she never went to sea again and was finally scrapped in 1946.

When we got to Canada I was selected and we climbed on a train and we went through the prairies for a three-day journey to a place called Caron which was in the middle of Saskatchewan. I did the primary course on an aeroplane called a Fairchild Cornell, a very nice aeroplane, and I was graded above average and I thought, 'That's splendid'. I was sent off to another school a service flying training school on Oxfords which was a proper RAF station further north in Saskatchewan. Well we survived there, I passed the wings exam and one morning, there were about twenty of us on the course, eight or ten of us were called into the office and they said, 'We've got more pilots than we know what to do with. You can be bomb-aimers or navigators, which do you wish to be?' I suppose I wasn't top grade in terms of my progress as a pilot and I was broken-hearted. I can remember crying. I thought I'd rather be a navigator than a bomb-aimer and so I was then put into a pool in Edmonton in Canada for two or three weeks and that's why I finished up in Canadian Flying Training Navigation School instead of RAF school.

I was at the Canadian school which was a small civilian school with not too many students. Most of them were Canadians but there were four English chaps. The senior English chap had been a corporal, he was also thirty-three years old and he was a school-master, so he was pronounced as being officer material and he got a commission. He was a pilot officer [while] the other three of us were sergeants and very pleased to be sergeants. We had this small parade there in Canada for some of the Canadian chaps getting their wings and their families had turned up from around Canada. We then were given our tickets, put on the train and back to the RAF central pool in Monkton in New Brunswick and from there we just waited for a ship which happened to be the *Mauretania*. It came up from New York with 9,000 Americans on board and we sailed for Liverpool.

This was just one of twenty-one Atlantic crossings by the *Mauretania* between April 1943 and March 1945, each time carrying thousands of American and Canadian troops bound for Britain and eventually for landings in Sicily, Normandy and the South of France. Her pre-war luxury was gone, replaced by a functional interior which crammed troops into every part of the ship.

We were two decks below the waterline. We were allowed half an hour or it may have been an hour a day on deck to have a breather and it was absolutely miserable. You slept on the tables and on the floors in various kit with dirty blankets. I was lucky because I had a hammock and I didn't have to suffer it but our meals? – we had a bucket of hot water for tea which was brought along three times a day and the other food we got was little cardboard cartons of American K-rations. You had a breakfast, you had a lunch and you had a supper and that's how we survived that particular voyage. We were very pleased to get to Liverpool. We travelled at about twenty-plus knots. They were too fast for the U-boats and they zig-zagged all the way out and all the way back. You knew when you were zig-zagging because the whole of the deck used to tilt as you altered course. It was a very safe way, considering the threat to the convoys, of moving across the ocean.

When we got off the ship we were sent to Harrogate, to the Majestic Hotel. All the services were really interested in was keeping you occupied until they got you into the training machine. There were various people who came round. I remember we were asked to volunteer for radar courses for night-fighters. I thought, 'I'm a navigator, I want to do proper navigation.' I didn't want particularly to be a specialist of that sort. After three or four weeks I got a posting and I was sent to Scotland to RAF West Freugh [near Stranraer] to a navigational advanced flying unit. There the training was devoted to getting you used to flying in the dark in a wartime zone, learning the procedures, the security and identification procedures and so forth as well as polishing up your navigation. It was pretty basic stuff. It was much of the same sort of practical navigational training that we were doing in Canada but in different weather, different atmosphere, black at night, no lights and that sort of thing.

I'd been at the school for three or four weeks, I'd done about eight or nine trips, quite short trips around the Irish Sea and up through the islands and so forth and I was summoned by the chief instructor into his office. I wondered what I'd done wrong and he said, 'Langston, Bomber Command have a new scheme. They are losing navigators at the advanced stages of crew training and they want to train a few up as spares on their own account, so we've chosen you. We're going to send you straight off to Bomber Command instead of the normal Operational Training Unit.' So I said, 'Thank you very much', and I got a train ticket and I was sent off to Winthorpe which was a Stirling heavy conversion unit near Newark.

I was trained on a one-to-one basis by this chap, Jim Warwick, who had just completed a tour. He had just won a DFC and he was the new station radar officer. In fact he was killed with Guy Gibson. I was on the same raid they were lost on a couple of months later. He taught me everything about navigating a four-engined bomber.

One experience while at Winthorpe showed John how dangerous flying could be.

> The second day I was at Winthorpe I was stood outside this hut where they had all this radar equipment that I was going to have to learn about and a Stirling at about 3,000 or 4,000 feet was approaching the airfield. I was stood with two or three other air-crew who were experienced chaps and one said, 'Oh God, he's on fire.' He had a starboard engine on fire and he approached over-head and, as he reached the end, the wing burnt off. It came down and I saw this Stirling go nose-down straight on the perimeter track on the far side of the airfield from where I stood. And all you could say was, 'Well I hope that doesn't happen to me.'

John had completed all the necessary training and was passed fit for operations. It was now just a question of waiting around for a crew that needed a navigator.

> I filled in my time as a screen instructor at Winthorpe. I used to fly with anybody as a screen instructor on the radar sets. One morning they said, 'You'll be pleased we've got a crew for you.' This was a crew whose navigator had got them lost several times. They'd been together for quite a while on Wellingtons on the operational training unit and they liked their navigator even if he'd got them lost. Anyway, he was replaced and I took over. They looked at me a bit askance but we did two or three cross-countries very quickly one after the other, three days in a row and the crew accepted me. I mean, they had no option but I didn't get them lost flying around England. They were keen to get on and they liked me and I liked them and so there we were, we were deemed as fit as a crew.

John's pilot was Londoner Bill Gordon who had enlisted into the RAFVR in 1941. He trained in the United States and, initially, was kept there as an instructor before returning to the UK. When John joined the crew he found, coincidentally, that he had previously flown with Bill Gordon's bomb-aimer, Pat Shirley, in the USA.

> We went off to a Lancaster finishing school at Syerston which is near Nottingham. We had three days there to learn to fly a

Lancaster as opposed to a Stirling and having been deemed an operational crew we were put on a ten-ton truck to East Kirkby to join our first squadron, Number 630. It was summertime, it was hot. I'm not a superstitious person but we were bundled out as a crew. I stood there in the sun and all of a sudden I was covered in ladybirds, there must have been thirty or forty and I thought that must be a good sign of some sort. We went inside the head-quarters and I met the navigation leader of the squadron and he said, 'Let me give you a word of advice. Wing Commander Gibson will be around all the time and my advice to you is to steer clear of him. If you see him go and hide.' Guy Gibson, of Dam-busters' fame, was Wing Commander, Operations at Coningsby He was known to be forceful in his attacks, I think that's a tactful way of putting it, in his requirements of all those around him.

No. 630 Squadron was formed in November 1943 and was imme-diately thrown into the midst of the battle for Berlin. The squadron went on a total of ten operations in the last six weeks of 1943 but eight of them were to Berlin, a real baptism of fire. By the time John arrived for his first operational posting in July 1944 630 Squadron had established itself at the heart of 5 Group's Main Force.

This was to be the first test for the crew. It was essential that they worked together well both on the ground and in the air.

The thing was, as a crew you lived together in each other's laps. I mean you ate together, you slept in bunks or in beds side by side, you were part of a crew and that's the way you thought about things. Everything was geared to that and to operational effec-tiveness. There was a lot of willingness to learn the other chap's job. I wanted to know what the wireless operator did. It was important that you should. We used to help the gunners clean their guns and things. Navigators were never short of things to do. You were always preparing charts or one thing and another. In the evenings when you were stood down you went off to the pub together. A crew's a crew and you really thought you knew what all the other chaps thought about things. You knew what made them irritable, you knew what made them pleased, you knew you had to get on. You were dependent for your life on the effectiveness of the gunners. If you were being attacked, they in fact, gave the orders – fighter up your backside – and you were dependent on the bomb-aimer. You were dependent on everybody for doing their job effectively. And, of course, we were fortunate with the pilot Bill Gordon who was a splendid chap. He'd been a flying instructor in America, although he was just only a Flying Officer when I joined him.

John Langston gave us one of the most detailed and insightful descriptions of a typical briefing together with all other preparations needed to make a crew and aircraft ready for an operation.

At briefing, the first thing that you did was [that] each crew had its own table and the navigator had his charts laid out on the table and the crew would sit around so that they could see. And then on the stage in front of you the briefing officers would have a large map and they would show you the whole route, the timing, they would tell you what the target was, what the purpose of the raid was. The nature of the target; an oil target, or refinery, or munitions factory or railway yards, whatever it might have been. The next thing was that they would show you the other forces that were operating that night. They would show your time on target and where your Main Force would be at any point and you would see all the other targets that would be selected for operations. You would know what other forces were operating in that area.

The next thing was that they would run over the known defences. Navigators, on their charts, always plotted in beforehand the main defensive positions where they knew that the enemy had guns that were in good working order and the thing to do was to avoid them. Then they covered communications, frequencies for the wireless operators. So, it was a busy thing. The navigators started their briefing roughly two hours ahead of the rest of the crew and you probably had the bomb-aimer with you and the pilot. You did all your basic chart work then. You measured your distances, your own distances, you put the lines on the paper and so on and got all your maps sorted out. You got your astro-navigation charts and tables sorted. You got all your radio frequencies, radar frequencies and things worked out and you knew what radar chains were using, if it was LORAN or Gee, and, if you were navigating primarily on H2S, which was the search radar, then you would be looking at the shapes of towns and things so that you knew what to expect along route. It was a busy job.

Well the last half hour before take-off you would be having a flying meal usually. You always looked forward to your egg which was special and you'd probably get a third of a pint of milk and some toast or some marmalade or jam. It was always, always good. You'd have a fag and things like that and then once you'd had that meal you'd go off to the squadron flying clothing rooms and don your kit. As a navigator nobody ever helped you, that was one of the problems, you had a sextant you had a navbag full of maps and charts and all the kit, you had your helmet, you had your parachute pack to carry and I always used to complain bitterly that nobody would help me.

The navigator was really the secretary, he kept the log of the flight and whenever an incident occurred you would record it and mark it on your chart. If you saw an aeroplane shot down or one of the gunners reported, you put a mark on the chart and you annotated it in your log. So, you had a complete log, if there were new guns or some new pyrotechnics appeared. Anything of interest to the intelligence people you would record. So a lot of de-briefing was concerned with what came out of your log and the record of the flight. The other members of the crew – the bomb-aimer – would give detailed descriptions of the target and the gunners would give their interpretation, pilot and flight engineer would describe that particular flight as they saw it. It didn't take all that long because, by this time you were usually quite tired and keen to have a post-flight breakfast.

For John and the rest of the crew, who had spent most of their four-engined aircraft training in Stirlings, the Lancaster was still a fairly new experience and completely different from the Stirling.

The Stirling was a very spacious aeroplane. It was rather like flying in a submarine: it had height and width and it was altogether generously proportioned in terms of the crew. The first time I saw a Lancaster I climbed inside it and I thought this is a nice compact lovely aeroplane. But it was really very tight and tiny. There was no spare space anywhere. Once you were sat in your seat you really didn't want to get out and move about unless you abso-lutely had to. I thought it had plenty of power. Twice we came back on three engines all the way from the middle of Germany but it had all the power in the world.

On more than one occasion their aircraft was attacked by a German night-fighter.

Becoming a good crew you learned on the job very quickly. One of the first things that you had to do was deal with being attacked by a fighter. If you had good gunners and they said, 'Ah, I can see a fighter coming in' you used to wait until the gunner said he was coming in to 800 to 600 yards. At about 600 yards range on his gun-sight you then corkscrewed. The pilot put the aeroplane on its side, you immediately dived, 1,000 or 1,500, even 2,000 feet and then, at the bottom of the turn, the fighter couldn't hold his sights onto you, he'd stall out as your own turn increased, so then you'd corkscrew back in a figure of eight until you were on your original course and you hoped by this time that you'd thrown the fighter off. Our very first attack came on a raid backing up the invasion in Normandy. This was a night thing and the fighter came in and we started to corkscrew. I'd done a practice one but I'd never done one on operations before. I was not exactly prepared for it and my chart came off the table. I lost my rubber and pencil on the floor and my dividers and my navigation table became a mess. Apart from that I was trying to lean over it to hold the chart down as we went down and keep everything in order. I lost all sorts of bits of things on the floor of the plane. As we straightened out and finished the thing I was down grovelling around trying to find my pencil and my rubber. As I was getting it all back together – my intercom had been pulled out of its socket – my pilot was up there yelling, 'Navigator!' because he wanted a new course. After he yelled 'Navigator!' twice and he hadn't had a reply the Wireless Op looked round the corner and saw that I was on the floor grovelling around trying to get my things and he said to the crew, 'He's under his table'. I was sorted out for every raid after that but, going into the target, about three minutes before, some wit in the crew would say, 'Is Johnny under the table yet?'

You concentrated your mind. I always thought that being in the centre of the stream was the safest place to be in a bomber stream so I always worked hard to make sure that's where we stayed and let the fighters pick off the chaps on the outside. That was my theory, anyway. But having said all that, it was still a matter of luck. Looking back on it, you could be the smartest and most brilliant crew but if your number was up, it was up.

In the bomber stream you were always in the slipstream of the aeroplane in front of you. All of a sudden the whole of the aeroplane would shake and wobble as you flew into somebody's slipstream. It was just as well it was dark because it was probably less frightening that way. But, if the aeroplane started wobbling the rest of the crew would be very happy, they'd say, 'Ah we're in the stream'. And you'd stay in the middle, not get on the side and get picked off.

No. 630 Squadron was based at East Kirkby, east of Lincoln. It was in the centre of an area dense with airfields, including Metheringham, Spilsby and Woodhall Spa. East Kirkby was a satellite station of Coningsby where all the operational and administrative work was done. No. 630 shared the airfield with 57 Squadron, another Lancaster squadron.

I lived in a Nissen hut with the rest of the sergeant aircrew, the gunners, the flight engineer and the wireless op. Pat Shirley my bomb-aimer who was a flight lieutenant and Bill Gordon, my pilot, who was a flying officer were in a different Nissen hut near the Officers' Mess. It was pretty miserable conditions really and it probably sounds silly but my greatest desire was to get a commission in the Royal Air Force so as to get out of having to live in the Sergeants' Mess with rough uniforms and have some comfort. I thought that they lived in comfort compared to the squalor that we lived in. It wasn't all that different but that was one of my grounds for seeking a commission.

At East Kirkby our dispersal for our particular aeroplane, which was always R Roger, was in a farmyard on the western side of the airfield and it was literally beside the farmhouse. The farmer and his young daughter became very friendly with us and when we were on the first trip to Konigsburg the plum season was on and the farmer's wife came out with a basket of plums to give to the wireless operator for us to have on route. We were very pleased and off we took. Once we got to altitude and were going across the North Sea the wireless operator started eating the plums. He offered them around but people didn't want to move seats so he started eating them all himself. We went over the southern end of Sweden he was still eating plums. About twenty minutes after that he said, 'I don't feel very well, I think I'm going to have to go back to the Elsan.' We gave him an oxygen bottle and he moved down to the back end of the aeroplane as we were flying up the Baltic. He finally had to get out of his flying suit and sit on the Elsan and he wasn't fit to get back into his seat until we were just perhaps twenty minutes before the target. Then we got him back and he didn't live that one down, I assure you.

John was in the thick of the bomber offensive from the start of his tour. His first operation was a daylight raid on 31 July 1944 against railway yards at Joigny la Roche some 100 miles south-east of Paris.

We did twenty-five operations together of all sorts. Our first few operations were in support of the D Day landings in France and we were interdicting the battlefield, bombing railway targets and things like that. Then the V-1 bombs started raining down on London and we were, after our first four or five trips, moved up to the Pas de Calais area to bomb buzz-bomb sites and that was quite hectic too. We were in a force of, say, 200 aeroplanes on a single buzz-bomb site and you were as worried about the bombs from the aeroplane above you as the flak from below. But we did four or five of those targets and then, all of a sudden, the target system changed and we went back onto deep penetration raids into Germany.

It was a torrid time for the bomber offensive as the squadrons were being asked to keep up the pressure on tactical targets behind the Normandy beachhead while still attacking long range strategic targets in Germany, and this while all the time crews were being lost.

Crews were coming and going all the time, even in my time in 1944 we were losing several crews a week and so you were all treated very much the same as everybody else. There'd be a few experienced chaps, some might even be on second tours but, by and large, you didn't mix a lot with them, you didn't mix with other crews too much. When you had time off you all went out for a beer together in the evening and the rest of the time you were kept very busy.

We went to Munich twice, we went to Nuremburg twice, we went to Darmstadt twice. We went to the far end of the Baltic, to back up the Russians, to Königsburg. That was interesting because the Russians were at the gates of the city, they'd been advancing into Germany and we were all given waistcoats. You put it on over your flying suit and it said 'Ja Anglo komen'. The instructions were that if you had to bale out and you met a Russian that you raised your arm and you pointed at your chest and said 'Ja Anglo Komen', 'I am English', and you hoped that that worked. Those were twelve-hour trips.

The second time we were dropping mines in the canal between Konigsburg and the Baltic Sea. We were detached from Main Force as a specialist team. We were dropping on the radar, getting down to I think it was about 4,000 or 5,000 feet to drop the mines in this deep-water canal. We were flying along happily, we dropped our mines and, all of a sudden, Pat the bomb-aimer said 'look out' and all hell let loose. Anchored at the mouth to this canal was the *Lützow* which was a pocket battleship and there was an awful lot of highly coloured flak coming in our direction. We got out of that as quickly as possible and then we had another six hours back to the UK. We also did more mining up in the Kattegat, the deep-water channels which brought the U-boats down between Sweden and Denmark.

So, by this time we were getting to be quite an experienced operational crew. We did Wilhelmshaven and other targets in North Germany, Mönchengladbach – that was the raid Gibson was killed on. So we were there at East Kirkby until about November. We'd done twenty-five trips and my pilot, Flying Officer Bill Gordon, was now considered to be a highly experienced operational captain and he suddenly found himself an acting squadron leader. We were moved to 189 Squadron, which was a newly-formed squadron over at Fulbeck.

No. 189 Squadron had only been formed the previous month and had flown just one operation out of RAF Bardney before moving to Fulbeck which they shared with 49 Squadron for the rest of the war. The squadron was still building up to full strength and needed experienced crews.

We were rationed, because of the loss rate, to one trip every two to three weeks. By this time Bill was well respected and we began to get jobs like leading the force. It was quite a thing to be lead navigator for a force of 200 bombers. I also had some minor additional responsibilities. Remember, when I went to 189 I was still a sergeant and the squadron navigation officer was at least a flight lieutenant, so I used to get ancillary jobs to do such as check other people, new crews' logs and things like that. I used to fly with the wing commander, the Commanding Officer, occasionally when he was looking for a navigator so that gave me a bit of extra work.

While at 189 Squadron, John's commission came through.

The adjutant gave me two small bits of pilot officer's ribbon to sew onto my battledress and took my sergeant's stripes off my arms. I moved my kit from the one hut we were in with the rest of my mates, the rest of my sergeant mates from the crew, into the same hut with Pat Shirley the bomb-aimer. Bill Gordon, having risen to the extreme dizzy heights of being flight commander, had his own room, so he was on his own. When my commission came through the adjutant also gave me a railway ticket and he said, 'You can go to London and see some tailors and get a uniform made'. So I had the day off, went to London, went to some tailors whose address I'd been given and they made me a uniform on the spot. I went and had some lunch and came back later that day, and had a fitting. I stayed in some wretched guest-house for the night and went back and got my uniform on and proceeded to get the train back to Fulbeck wearing my pilot officer's uniform. I was pleased as Punch.

In practical terms it meant an extra half-crown a day, which was quite important. It meant that somebody brought me a jug of hot water in the morning to shave with which was an absolute luxury. It meant eating in the Officers' Mess as opposed to the Sergeants' Mess. There wasn't much difference in that except that I do remember that they trusted officers better than they trusted sergeants, because in the Officers Mess when you went in for lunch there was always a tray of glasses of milk and they trusted you to take one glass and behave like a gentlemen and not steal anybody else's whereas in the Sergeants' Mess they didn't trust you with milk at all.

John ended his first tour with a long-range operation against an oil refinery at Politz, near what is now the Poland/Czech Republic border, on the night of 13 January 1945. He was looking forward to some well-deserved leave.

> We finished our last trip on 189 Squadron – we went to some oil refinery. The following morning we were up bright and spritely. My bomb-aimer had a motorbike and I was on the back of it and we were buzzing around the station. Bill Gordon came out of his office and said 'Guess what', and Pat said to him, 'What?' and Bill said, 'The CO of 617 Squadron has phoned up and he would like us to join him, what do you think?' And Pat looked at him and said, 'Sir', be off with you' – or rather more vehemently! So, we got the crew together and the following day we all packed our bags and went off to 617. That was going from squalor to luxury. The officers were accommodated in the Petwood Hotel, which was a palatial pre-war building although we slept six or eight to a room.

John was officially posted to 617 Squadron on 6 February 1945 along with the rest of the crew. This coincided with a period of bad weather. Very few operations could take place and many of those that did were cancelled.

By this time 617 Squadron had a new commanding officer. Group Captain Johnny Fauquier was a vastly experienced Canadian pilot who had already been awarded two DSOs and a DFC. Older than most of the fresh faced youngsters who joined up in 1939, Fauquier was already thirty years old. Rapidly proving his capabilities as a bomber pilot he was promoted to wing commander and took command of 405 Squadron in 1943. At the end of his tour he was promoted to air commodore but voluntarily reverted to group captain and took command of 617 Squadron in December 1944, replacing the tour-expired James Tait.

John and the crew were very flattered to have been chosen for 617 Squadron.

> I guess we had a bit of hubris. I guess we were quite pleased to be selected and after all it was quite an honour to be selected and I think we appreciated that. One of the reasons we went, I suppose, is that you can talk any young fool into anything if you pat them

on the back enough. And, of course, it was an elite squadron, there's no doubt about that.

But then of course, having got on the squadron, 617 was a squadron that always had unique targets and they always required deep training, so for the first three or four weeks we were on the squadron we were doing nothing but going off to the ranges and dropping practice bombs. We had a new bomb-sight to cope with, the Stabilised Automatic Bomb-sight, the SABS. We were the only squadron equipped with them. We had to get a specific score on the ranges and I think it must have taken us eight or nine sorties or maybe more before we got down to the bombing level averages required and were deemed to be operational. At the same time Bill Gordon had moved over to 617 as the B Flight Commander. That was quite a thing because by then, having been cleared, we were dropping Tallboys – Barnes Wallis' smaller deep penetration bomb.

John remembers his first operation with 617 Squadron very well. It was an attack on the Bielefeld viaduct.

Well, it sticks in my mind because here was Bill Gordon as B Flight Commander leading the force onto the viaduct. This time, instead of leading 200 aeroplanes we were just the squadron with our own fighter escort. But this was the raid before Calder dropped the Grand Slam and we were a Tallboy raid. With our Tallboys we had some close hits but we didn't get the viaduct. I think it was two days later that Calder finally got the first Grand Slam to arrive on the squadron. He dropped it and the viaduct came down. It was an important target because, like all the Grand Slam raids, we were taking out bridges so that the Germans couldn't bring up fuel on the railway lines to support their forces in France.

The Lancaster was a different kettle of fish on 617. For the really big bombs like the Grand Slams the mid-upper turrets had been taken out, all the ammunition had been taken out, all the heavy radio equipment and radar equipment was missing. We just had three VHF sets, one for the fighter frequency, one for the bomber frequency and one for air traffic. We flew without the upper turret so we had a basic crew of five. What is interesting is [that], with the bomb doors removed, the Grand Slam itself was wider than the width of the fuselage so it was slung externally underneath with a couple of arms to hold it in position. We flew with probably two thirds tanks to reduce weight and we had the Lincoln under-carriage in order to carry the thing. We had a reinforced main spar in the centre to take the weight of the bomb. But all said and done, the total all-up weight with no turrets, no ammunition, no nothing else was only about 6,000 pounds heavier than the ordinary Lancaster with full tanks and a 12,000-pound bomb load. So, it was not all that dramatic except that once you got airborne then you noticed that the plane was taking the strain and the wingtips actually moved up about six or eight inches each side, it was quite remarkable to see.

We had the latest mark of Merlin and were allowed several extra pounds of boost on take-off but you could only have that on for, I think, about ten or twelve seconds once you were off the ground and the engineer was always keen to throttle back to keep his engines healthy. Then it was a long slow climb up to altitude. We would bomb from about 17,000 feet with the Grand Slam. You leapt upwards and it was noticeable, this leap, and, furthermore, the wings having bent upwards came back into their proper position.

On 9 April 1945 John flew on an operation to attack the U-boat pens of Hamburg.

Towards the end of the war we were doing a lot of daylight raids. I remember coming out of the U-boat pens at Harburg, south of Hamburg. We'd gone through the target, we'd bombed very suc-cessfully with a Tallboy and I could see in the distance the Mustangs of our fighter escort because, on 617, we didn't really have any turrets on the aeroplanes; we just relied on a fighter escort above us. I saw a Mustang on his nose trying to catch another aeroplane and the other aeroplane disappeared. It was a Messerschmitt 262, the first German twin-jet fighter. It banked around and headed towards us and in our little gaggle we all tightened up because other crews were also watching this too. I could see a wing-tip coming in, I was stood up behind the pilot having a good look, and I could see wing-tips coming in closer and closer. And then out of this 262, this all happened in a few seconds, I saw two little black dots. And it suddenly dawned on me that these were rockets and he'd loosed them. I have to confess that as they came over the top of us I ducked. But they hit the Lanc that was next to us flown by an Australian called Gavin and it was quite extraordinary. One of the rockets must have missed but one hit his starboard outer engine and all it did was knock the casing off it and the engine continued to rotate and fly and there he was with a naked engine and the aeroplane was still going along.

Almost every man who flew on Bomber Command operations had, at best, some dicey moments. John remembers two specific times when things didn't go strictly according to plan.

The worst memories that I had on ops were really of minor temporary failures in navigation. I can remember we went to Swinemunde and we were coming out over the coast and we were picked up by a fighter. We corkscrewed as it came in on the attack and as we straightened up, we thought we'd lost it. But, it came in again and it did this three times to the extent that Bill Gordon actually had blood blisters on his hands. Every time we really corkscrewed the compasses fell apart because you toppled the gyros in the master unit and the things were upside down. When we finally shook this fighter off Bill said to me, 'I want a course for home.' I said, 'I don't know where we are.' He said I must draw up a course and I was there fiddling around trying to get the compasses back together. I knew that we were over in that part of the North Sea, I just didn't know where we were to within 30 or 40 miles. All of a sudden there was bang-bang-bang-bang-bang and I thought 'thank goodness'. We were in range of the heavy flak out of Heligoland and it was underneath us. So I restarted my plot from Heliogoland and gave him a course home which I invented. So that was one little occasion.

The other occasion was when we were on one of these twelve-hour trips out to the far end of the Baltic. On the way home, we got back into Gee range over the North Sea to fix our position and I took a fix and put it on my chart and put the time against it and, of course, six minutes later I looked at my watch and thought, 'Oh! I must take another fix', and I put another one on the chart. The fix was alright, but the time was all wrong and I took one again. I hadn't realised that I was so tired that I'd forgotten to wind my watch and I had these fixes from the radar going across the North Sea all with the same time against them. It suddenly dawned on me what I had done. So then I had the embarrassment to ask somebody else in the crew if they had a watch which had something like the right time on it and could they give me the time. That took some living down.

On 22 March Bill Gordon's crew dropped their first Grand Slam bomb. This successful operation destroyed the bridge over the River Weser at Nienberg in Northern Germany.

Grand Slam bombs were in short supply at this time and, from the Nienberg operation onwards, Johnny Fauquier made a somewhat unpopular decision to insist crews brought their bombs back if they weren't needed on an operation. The first four crews dropped their bombs at Nienberg and, when Fauquier saw that the bridge was destroyed, he ordered the other aircraft to take their bombs home.

Fauquier said he wouldn't want to do it again but he had aeroplanes that went in on some of these bridges and just the first four dropped their bombs. If they took the target out we went home with the bombs. He did that the first time and he said, 'Well it was a bit of a gamble', but of course we had a fighter escort and the war was right at the end.

We dropped our first one, and the next day two crews were sent off to the English Steel company in Sheffield where the bombs were made. The idea was to pep up the workforce to make some more because the Grand Slams were so difficult they were literally being handmade one at a time. We put on our best blues and we all went off to Sheffield from Woodhall Spa. We were greeted by the board of directors who saw that these bold aviators had come to their factory and we were given large whiskies. Then we were taken down into the casting room which was a huge amphitheatre really where they were actually pouring the steel into the sand mould for the main bomb casing. But this room had a sort of mezzanine around it about twenty feet off the ground and it was full of Russian flags with the hammer and sickle on them. And either side and in the centre was another great big sheet. On this great big sheet it said 'God bless Uncle Joe', Joe Stalin of course. We looked at each other and we thought this is very odd, but we really didn't understand the politics of Sheffield and the local workers. So we watched them pour the casting of this bomb and then they moved us into the next room where a bomb had been poured two or three days before and had cooled sufficiently to be worked on and it was lying on its side and, of course, this bomb, the back end where you put in the explosive and everything was quite a big hole and they had two quite small men there with pneumatic hammers. [Their] job was to go around and see if there were any flaws in the cast. And where [they] saw anything, in order to get a smooth explosion, [they] had to hammer it out with [a] pneumatic hammer. Well, if you think of yourself being inside a steel casing like this they could only do it for about fifteen or twenty seconds and then they had to pull this poor chap out by the back legs. They waited for a bit and put the next one in to carry on the process. So this poor man came out. He was as small as a jockey and he was stood behind me shaking and I gave him a cigarette and I lit it. He took the cigarette and said, 'What do you do?' and I said, 'I drop them'. He looked at me and he said, 'What do they pay you?' and I said, 'Fourteen shillings and sixpence a day'. He said, 'You're a fool, I get ten quid a week for doing this', and that's the truth and I've been dining out on that story since the day it happened.

There came a time when John was aware that the war was nearing its end. On 16 April 1945 eighteen aircraft undertook an operation against the *Lützow* in the harbour at Schweinemunde, a port on the Baltic coast near the German/Polish border.

All our operations were daylights and we had air superiority. We had we had our own fighter escort force. Some of the targets I even pondered, 'Gosh, I wouldn't want to get shot down at this stage of the war' because I wasn't sure that this was worth a candle. I remember when we went to the *Lützow*. We eventually sank the *Lützow* and one of the aeroplanes ahead of us got a direct hit and went down and I thought, 'Well the war's over, what rotten luck'.

This was the Lancaster of Squadron Leader Powell which received such heavy damage that the port wing fell off and it spiralled into the ground, killing all the crew.

John went on one final operation for the squadron, a successful daylight raid to bomb the coastal guns at Heligoland on 19 April.

Bill Gordon's crew took no part in 617 Squadron's final operation of the war when sixteen aircraft were sent to bomb Hitler's mountain retreat of Berchtesgaden in Bavaria. However, they were one of five crews sent to Germany on 8 May 1945.

VE Day was an interesting day for us because we all flew off to Germany and we picked up prisoners of war. We picked up about ten or fifteen and stuck them in the back of the Lancaster and they just lay on mats or rugs. We flew them back to Dunsfold in Surrey. And as we came back we flew in low over the white cliffs of Dover. All these poor chaps who'd been prisoners since 1939 and 1940 came up into the cockpit to see the UK for the first time. And they started to cry and we started to cry and that was really quite a moving experience. Then we flew back to Woodhall Spa and we all went down to the Spa Hotel which was our drinking haunt there to drink a few beers and celebrate the day and the occasion in the grounds of the Spa Hotel. They also had an airborne division in Woodhall Spa. They occupied the Golf Hotel there. But the Spa Hotel had their Horsa glider that they'd practised all their landing drills in for evacuating the thing. The Army had set it alight, so we all danced around this blazing Horsa glider with pints of beer, so that was my VE Day.

In 1944, at the Quebec conference, British Prime Minister Winston Churchill proposed to transfer many squadrons, after the end of the war in Europe, from Bomber Command to the Far East to step up the war against Japan. No. 617 Squadron was earmarked to go but the dropping of the atomic bombs on Hiroshima and Nagasaki, and the subsequent surrender of Japan, precluded this move.

John Langston, however, was posted away from 617 Squadron with the rest of the crew on 29 March 1945

After VE Day 617 was earmarked to go to the Far East. Eventually they would go as far as India. But the rest of us on the squadron were all sent off to 15 Squadron at Mildenhall and we formed a bomb development unit. We were dropping Tallboys and Grand Slams on the various buzz-bomb targets left over and the German V-2 and V-3 targets with all their reinforced concrete in in Northern France just to check the penetration qualities. But we were there for a week or two and we dropped a few Tallboys and a lot of 2,000-pounders I remember. And Bill Gordon, my pilot, said to me, 'I think we can do something better than this, let's see if we can get into Transport Command.' So Bill and I left the crew, or left Pat Shirley the bomb-aimer, the rest of the crew, I think, had disappeared, and we went off and converted onto Yorks and went into 46 Group. I spent the next six months flying out to Calcutta twice a month rather like a civil airliner for trooping.

John Langston stayed in Bomber Command after the war, eventually becoming commanding officer of 49 Squadron on Vickers Valiants. John was Captain of the Valiant's final ever bombing sortie on 9 December 1964 and eventually retired from the RAF with the rank of air commodore. At the time of writing John is President of the 617 Squadron Association.

Pilot Officer John Langston – Operations at 617 Squadron

- 9 March 1945 – Bielefeld – Viaduct. Mission abandoned due to bad weather over the target.
- 21 March 1945 – Bremen – Arbergen railway bridge. Successful operation as target heavily damaged and put out of use.
- 22 March 1945 – Nienburg – Railway bridge. Successful operation as the bridge was destroyed.
- 23 March 1945 – Bremen – Railway bridge. Successful operation. Target destroyed.
- 6 April 1945 – Ijmuiden – Shipping. Mission aborted due to heavy cloud over target.
- 7 April 1945 – Ijmuiden – Shipping. Improved weather meant that the operation went ahead with several hits being recorded.
- 9 April 1945 – Hamburg – U-boat pens. Successful operation. Several hits severely damaged the pens.
- 13 April 1945 – Schweinemunde – Shipping. Bad weather caused the operation to be aborted.
- 15 April 1945 – Schweinemunde – Shipping. Mission aborted due to heavy cloud over the target.
- 16 April 1945 – Schweinemunde – Shipping. Finally the improving weather allowed the attack to take place. The German cruiser *Lützow*, originally the *Deutschland* but renamed, was caught in the Kaiserfahrt, the narrow canal leading to the Baltic, and sunk with several near misses and a single hit.

- 19 April 1945 – Heligoland – Coastal gun batteries. Successful operation against this German island in the North Sea. Guns hit with Tallboys on this eighteenth and final operation against the island.

John Langston was posted to 15 Squadron from 617 Squadron on 29 May 1945

Appendix

Locations of 617 Squadron Targets

Albert is in the Somme department in Picardie in northern France. The target was an aircraft factory.

Altenfjord is in the northern tip of Norway and was where the Germans had a major naval base at Kåfjord. *Tirpitz* was moored here and was attacked twice before being moved further south to Tromsø.

Angoulême is in Poitou-Charentes, south-western France. The target was an explosives works.

Antheor Viaduct is on the Cote d'Azure in southern France just to the east of St Raphael. It forms part of the coastal rail link between France and Italy and as such was an important means of moving men and equipment in the region.

Aquata Scrivia is in the Piedmont region of north-western Italy sixty-two miles south-east of Turin. The target was a power station.

Arnsberg is in the North Rhine-Westphalia region of western Germany. The target was a viaduct.

Berchesgarden-Wachenfels is in the Bavarian Alps near the Austrian border and the home of Adolf Hitler.

Bergen is on Norway's west coast and the targets were U-boat pens and shipping in the harbour.

Bergerac is in the Dordogne department in south-western France. The target was an explosives factory.

Bielefeld Viaduct is near Munster in north-western Germany.

Blida is in Algeria about twenty-eight miles south-west of Algiers. 617 Lancasters were re-fuelled and rearmed before making the return trip, bombing further targets.

Boulogne is a port in the Pas-de-Calais in northern France. E-boat pens and other harbour installations were the targets.

Brest is on the Atlantic coast of Brittany in north-western France. The target was the submarine pens.

Brunswick is in Lower Saxony in the northern Germany. During the war it was a centre for aircraft production.

Clermont Ferrand is a large industrial city in the Auvergne region in central France. The target was the Michelin Tyre factory.

Creil is in the Oise department of northern France. The target was a major ammunition dump.

Dams Raid

> **Sorpe Dam** is in the west of Germany near the small town of Sundern in the German district of Hochsauerland in North Rhine-Westphalia.

> **Eder Dam** is near the small town of Waldeck in northern Hesse, Germany. It lies at the northern edge of the Kellerwald.

> **Möhne Dam** is part of an artificial lake in North Rhine-Westphalia, some twenty-eight miles east of Dortmund.

Dortmund-Ems canal is just south of Munster in north-western Germany. The target was an aqueduct.

Dreis is in western Germany and the target was the Arbergen Bridge.

Etaples is just west of Boulogne in northern France. A railway bridge was the target.

Farge is a port in Bremen and the U-boat pens was the target.

Genoa is a Mediterranean port in north-western Italy. The target was the railway line.

Hamburg is on the Elbe river in northern Germany. The target was the U-boat pens.

Heligoland is two islands in the south-eastern North Sea just off the German coast. The target was coastal gun batteries.

Ijmuiden is north-west of Amsterdam in the Netherlands. The target was shipping.

Juvisy-sur-Orge is in the Île-de-France in northern France, 18 km south-east of Paris. Here, 617 attacked the railway marshalling yards.

Kembs. The target was the Rhine Barrage in the Haut Rhine region of Alsace.

Keroman was the submarine base at Lorient in southern Brittany in western France.

la Chapelle-du-Mont-de-France is in the Saône-et-Loire department in the Burgundy region of eastern France. The marshalling yards were the target.

la Pallice is the name of the harbour at la Rochelle in western France where there were U-boat pens.

Leghorn/Livorno is a port on the Tyrrhenian Sea on the western coast of Tuscany, Italy. The target was the docks.

le Havre is a port in the upper Normandy region of northern France. The harbour included E-boat pens.

Liège is a large Belgian city to the east of the country. The target was the armament works.

Limoges is in the Limousin region of western-central France. The target was the Gnome-Rhône aero engine works.

Lyon, traditionally spelt Lyons in English, is a city in east-central France in the Rhône-Alpes region. An aero engine facility was attacked.

Mailly is in the Burgundy region of eastern France. During the war here was a military camp here that was marked by 617 for Main Force to attack.

Milan is in the Lombardy region of Northern Italy. The sortie was to drop leaflets over the city. These types of operations were known as Nickels.

Mimoyecques is in the Pas-de- Calais in northern France and was the site for the V-3 'Supergun'.

Munich is in Bavaria in southern Germany and was a very long range attack for the squadron.

Nienburg is on the Weser river in the Lower Saxony region of Germany. The target was a bridge.

Oslofjord is in south-eastern Norway with Oslo at its northern end. The targets were German cruisers.

Pölitz is in north-western Poland. The synthetic oil plant was the target.

Poortershaven is west of Rotterdam in the Netherlands and U-boat pens were built here.

Rilly–la-Montagne is in the Marne region of north-eastern France. The railway tunnel there was used as a storage depot for V-1 Flying Bombs. 617 were to attack a number of V-1 sites during 1944/45

Rotterdam is in the province of South Holland in the western Netherlands. During the war this major harbour housed E-boat pens.

San Polo D'enza is in the Emilia-Romagna region of Northern Italy, located about forty-four miles west of Bologna and about twelve miles south-west of Reggio Emilia. The target was a power station.

Saumur is in the Loire in western France. A tunnel and rail bridge were the targets.

Siracourt is in the Pas-de-Calais region of northern France and was one of the launch sites for the V-1 flying bombs.

St Cyr is to the west of Paris in France. The target was a German signals equipment depot.

St Étienne is a city in eastern central France. It is located in the Massif Central, thirty miles south-west of Lyon. The target was a needle bearing factory.

Schweinemunde is on the Baltic Sea in north-west Poland. The targets were the German heavy cruiser *Prinz Eugen* and the 'pocket battleship' *Lützow*.

Toulouse The targets were aircraft factories on the outskirts of this southern French city.

Tromsø in Norway was where the *Tirpitz* was moved after 617's earlier attacks. It was to be her final resting place following 617's third attack.

Urft Dam is in North Rhine-Westphalia in western Germany.

Watten is near Dunkirk in northern France and was a launch site for V-2 rocket attacks.

Westkapelle is on the island of Walcheren on the south-western tip of the Netherlands. The operation was to breach the sea wall and flood the surrounding countryside.

Wizernes is just to the south-west of St Omer in northern France. The Germans were building a V–weapons launch site when 617 attacked.

Woippy is in the Moselle department in Lorraine in north-eastern France. The target was an aero engine works.

Yagodnik is in north-western Russia. 617 flew from here during their first operation against the *Tirpitz*.

Index